The Promise of Cybersecurity

Cybersecurity

From Prevention to Response: Building a Fortified Cyber Environment

Olivia Martinez

Table of Contents

INTRODUCTION

In an increasingly digital world, the importance of cybersecurity cannot be overstated. "The Promise of Cybersecurity: From Prevention to Response: Building a Fortified Cyber Environment" delves into the intricate landscape of cyber threats and the measures necessary to safeguard our digital lives. This book is designed to be a comprehensive guide for both novices and experts, offering insights into cybersecurity's evolution, current state, and future.

From understanding fundamental concepts to exploring advanced defense mechanisms, this book covers every aspect of cybersecurity. You will learn about the various types of cyber threats, including malware, phishing, and advanced persistent threats, and how to protect against them. It also addresses the critical role of a robust incident response plan and the legal and ethical considerations in the field.

Moreover, the book explores the challenges and opportunities presented by emerging technologies such as AI, quantum computing, and cloud services. Examining real-world case studies and offering practical strategies provides readers with actionable steps to enhance their cybersecurity posture.

Whether you are an IT professional seeking to bolster your organization's defenses or an individual aiming to protect personal data, "The Promise of Cybersecurity" is your essential resource for building a fortified cyber environment. Join us on this journey to understand, prevent, and respond to cyber threats in our interconnected world.

CHAPTER I

Getting Started to Cybersecurity

The Importance of Cybersecurity in the Modern World

The digital era has completely changed how we live, work, and communicate in today's connected world. Technology is advancing at an unprecedented rate, transforming sectors and spawning a global digital economy with unmatched convenience and efficiency. Digital assets and data security are crucial since the digital revolution has also brought severe cybersecurity issues.

The pervasiveness of internet-connected gadgets, from laptops and smartphones to smart household appliances and industrial control systems, characterizes the current digital landscape. The Internet of Things (IoT), which is the term used to describe this widespread proliferation of devices, is a complex network of interconnected systems that enable smooth data exchange and communication. Although there are many advantages to this connectedness, there are also weaknesses that bad actors could use.

The exponential rise in cyber threats is one of the main factors contributing to the growing significance of cybersecurity. Simple viruses and worms have given way to more complex and focused cyberattacks coordinated by nation-states, hacktivist organizations, and organized crime syndicates. Cybersecurity experts face distinct problems from various threats, such as ransomware, phishing, malware, and distributed denial-of-service (DDoS) assaults.

Malicious software, or malware, is a general term for various destructive programs intended to compromise and compromise computer systems. Trojan horses, worms, and viruses are popular forms of malware that may spread quickly and do a great deal of harm. A particularly sneaky kind of malware called ransomware encrypts a victim's data and demands payment to unlock it. This can result in significant financial losses and disruptions to operations. The necessity for solid cybersecurity measures has become more apparent due to ransomware attacks' rising frequency and sophistication.

Another common cyber threat is phishing, which uses psychological tricks to trick people into disclosing private information. Phishing attacks usually entail impersonating a trustworthy website or email to deceive the target into divulging personal information like credit card numbers or passwords. Phishing is booming even with increased awareness because of its constantly changing strategies and attackers' ease of imitating reputable organizations and brands.

DDoS assaults, on the other hand, try to interfere with online services by flooding them with traffic. These assaults can potentially destroy networks, internet services, and websites, causing significant downtime and monetary damage. The availability of DDoS-for-hire services has further complicated the cybersecurity environment by making it more straightforward for even inexperienced people to initiate these attacks.

Individuals need to be mindful of cybersecurity and practice good hygiene. Cyberattack risk can be considerably decreased by implementing easy procedures like creating strong, one-of-a-kind passwords, turning on multi-factor authentication, and being alert for phishing attempts. People must understand their responsibility as digital citizens to protect their personal information and support a safe online community.

In conclusion, it is impossible to exaggerate the significance of cybersecurity in the present world. While there is never-before-seen potential in the digital world, there are also significant risks in the shape of constantly changing cyber threats. Strong cybersecurity safeguards are more important than ever as nation-state actors and hackers develop more advanced assault techniques. We can create a fortified digital environment that allows us to enjoy the advantages of the digital age while protecting our assets, privacy, and national security by investing in state-of-the-art technologies, promoting a culture of security awareness, and prioritizing cybersecurity at all levels.

Historical Context and Evolution of Cybersecurity

Since its start, the discipline of cybersecurity has seen a significant evolution due to the swift progress of technology and the growing complexity of cyber threats. Knowing the background and development of cybersecurity over time offers essential insights into how we got to the current state of digital security and identifies the turning points that have shaped its advancement.

When computers were first invented, cybersecurity was not a top priority. The original computers were segregated devices with sparse networking, mainly employed for specialized military and scientific purposes. The primary security protocols concentrated more on access control and physical security than safeguarding against online attacks. But as computer networks advanced, the necessity of cybersecurity became increasingly apparent.

The development of the Advanced Research Projects Agency Network (ARPANET), the forerunner to the current internet, in the 1970s is considered the birthplace of cybersecurity. A small number of computers were connected by the ARPANET, allowing researchers to share resources and data. When Bob Thomas produced the Creeper virus in 1971—often regarded as the first computer virus—the network's early flaws were apparent. This virus only showed the message "I'm the creeper: catch me if you can," so it was comparatively safe, but it did show how harmful code could spread over a network.

Ray Tomlinson, also credited with creating email, created the first antivirus application, Reaper, in reaction to the Creeper virus. Reaper was meant to remove the infection. This started a cat-and-mouse game between people who created viruses and those attempting to stop them, laying the groundwork for contemporary cybersecurity procedures.

The adoption of encryption standards was another significant development in the 1990s. The Advanced Encryption Standard (AES) was adopted in 2001 due to the Data Encryption Standard (DES), created in the 1970s, being viewed as inadequate. AES became the industry standard for protecting sensitive data and communications because it offered more excellent encryption.

The prevalence of malware in the late 1990s and early 2000s contributed to the growth of the antivirus sector. Enterprises such as Symantec, McAfee, and Kaspersky Lab surfaced, providing software solutions for identifying and eliminating viruses, worms, and other nasty applications. The quick growth of malware put antivirus software to the test regularly, requiring upgrades and enhancements.

A new age of cybersecurity concerns began at the turn of the millennium with the emergence of highly skilled cyberattacks and the internet's commercialization. One of the most well-known events occurred in 2000 when the Love Bug virus (ILOVEYOU) spread via email, costing billions of dollars in damages globally. The significance of email security and user awareness in stopping the spread of malware was highlighted by this incident.

The danger landscape changed along with the digital landscape. Advanced persistent threats (APTs) are long-term, targeted attacks that nation-states or organized crime groups usually plan. They first surfaced in the mid-2000s. The 2010 discovery of the Stuxnet worm, directed toward Iran's nuclear facilities, is a noteworthy illustration of the potential for actual cyberattack harm.

The significance of cybersecurity will only increase going forward. Because our digital world is interconnected, maintaining the security of our data and systems is essential to society's ability to function. Through historical reflection and proactive threat mitigation, we can create a more secure digital environment where the advantages of technology are realized without jeopardizing our privacy and safety.

Understanding Cyber Threats

Cyber threats are a global problem that affects people, companies, and governments everywhere in the digital era. To fully appreciate the complexities of cybersecurity and the impact of these harmful activities, it is necessary to comprehend the many forms of cyber threats and review case studies of notable cyber-attacks. The field of cyber threats is broad and includes a variety of strategies and tools that cybercriminals employ to break into systems, steal confidential data, and exploit weaknesses.

Malicious software, or malware, is one of the most prevalent categories of cyber threats. A wide range of malicious software, including Trojan horses, worms, viruses, ransomware, spyware, and adware, are called malware. Viruses are made to attach to and propagate throughout computers by attaching themselves to legitimate files, frequently harming data and system integrity. Like viruses, worms are self-replicating programs that propagate without a host file, which often causes system slowdowns and network congestion. Trojans pose as trustworthy software, but once launched, they provide hackers with illegal access, allowing them to steal data or install other malware.

A hazardous type of malware is ransomware, which encrypts a victim's files and requests payment—typically in cryptocurrency—to unlock them. When the WannaCry outbreak struck in May 2017, it was one of the most prominent ransomware assaults. Using a Microsoft Windows vulnerability, WannaCry quickly expanded worldwide, impacting over 200,000 systems in 150 countries. Surgery cancellations and interruptions in healthcare services resulted from the significant damage to critical infrastructure, which included the National Health Service (NHS) of the United Kingdom. The incident clarified the importance of regular software upgrades and strong cybersecurity defenses.

Another common cyber threat is phishing, which uses social engineering to trick people into disclosing private information like credit card numbers, usernames, and passwords. Phishing attacks frequently take the shape of phony emails or websites that mimic reliable sources. Phishing is still quite successful because of its sophisticated attacks and psychological manipulation, even with increased awareness of the practice. One well-known instance of phishing was the 2016 Democratic National Committee (DNC) hack. Thousands of private emails were leaked due to hackers tricking DNC personnel into giving their email credentials through spear-phishing emails. This hack proved the importance of strict email security procedures and had significant political repercussions.

Distributed denial of service (DDoS) attacks aim to interfere with online services by flooding them with so much traffic that legitimate users cannot access them. These assaults have the potential to seriously impair operations and finances by focusing on websites, online services, and even whole networks. Primary DNS service Dyn was the target of one of the worst DDoS assaults in history in October 2016. Twitter, Netflix, and Reddit were among the popular websites and services affected by the attack, carried out by a botnet of infected Internet of Things devices. The Dyn assault demonstrated the weaknesses on the Internet of Things devices and the possibility of severe disruptions from DDoS attacks.

Cyberattacks that are more sophisticated and specifically targeted are known as Advanced Persistent Threats (APTs), and they are frequently conducted by highly organized criminal gangs or nation-state actors. APTs are long-term, covert operations designed to steal confidential data or jeopardize vital infrastructure. The 2010 discovery of the Stuxnet worm makes it one of the most notorious APTs. Stuxnet primarily targeted Iran's nuclear installations, causing harm to uranium enrichment centrifuges. Most people agree that Israel and the United States worked together to create Stuxnet to obstruct Iran's nuclear development. Because of Stuxnet's advanced design and ability to take advantage of several zero-day vulnerabilities, the employment of cyberweapons for geopolitical objectives has significantly increased.

Creating successful cybersecurity plans requires understanding the many cyber threats and the lessons learned from significant cyberattacks. Specific defenses must be put in place to lessen the impact of each kind of threat. Each threat poses different difficulties. Case studies of substantial cyberattacks, like the Equifax breach, WannaCry, the DNC breach, the Dyn DDoS attack, and Stuxnet, provide insightful insights into the significance of proactive security measures, timely upgrades, and effective incident response strategies.

Being aware and cautious is crucial as cyber threats are constantly changing. Businesses need to invest in cutting-edge security solutions, conduct frequent security audits, and encourage a security-aware culture among staff members. People also need to take accountability for their online safety by following best practices in cybersecurity, such as creating secure passwords, turning on multi-factor authentication, and being wary of shady emails and links. We may create a more secure digital environment and defend ourselves against the constant risks of the cyber world by comprehending the nature of cyber threats and learning from previous instances.

The Promise of a Secure Cyber Environment

Cybersecurity has become essential for safeguarding private information in the modern digital age. Strong cybersecurity measures are becoming increasingly important as our reliance on digital platforms and networked devices increases. The numerous advantages of solid cybersecurity, such as protecting private data, preserving the integrity of our digital exchanges, and protecting sensitive information, hold the promise of a safe cyber environment.

Strong cybersecurity protects against online dangers, including ransomware, phishing, malware, and advanced persistent threats. Robust security policies can be put in place by enterprises to stop unauthorized users from accessing their networks and systems, protecting sensitive data from loss or alteration. Maintaining information availability, confidentiality, and integrity—three essential cybersecurity tenets—requires this protection. This entails safeguarding client information, financial records, intellectual property, and other vital assets for firms that could harm their finances and reputation in case of a breach.

Protecting private information is one of the main advantages of solid cybersecurity. In a time when cyberattacks and data breaches are happening more frequently, protecting personal data is crucial. Good cybersecurity practices reduce exposure by ensuring that private information, including credit card details, social security numbers, and medical records, is encrypted and maintained securely. This protection is necessary for both individuals and businesses handling sensitive data because these businesses are legally required to protect the data of their clients under several laws and guidelines, including the Health Insurance Portability and Accountability Act (HIPAA) in the US and the General Data Protection Regulation (GDPR) in the EU.

Consumers and clients are also more likely to trust in a safe cyber environment. People and businesses are more willing to transact and connect online when they have confidence that their data is secure. This trust is especially crucial since sensitive information is often exchanged on e-commerce platforms, banking institutions, and healthcare providers. Businesses can improve their brand, draw in and keep clients, and obtain a competitive edge by showcasing their dedication to cybersecurity. To establish and preserve trust, robust cybersecurity is essential, and trust is a fundamental element of the digital economy.

Furthermore, maintaining an organization's operational continuity depends heavily on robust cybersecurity measures. Cyberattacks can cause severe disruptions, including lost productivity, downtime, and financial losses. For example, ransomware attacks can completely shut down an organization's systems and important files unless a ransom is paid. Organizations can reduce the danger of these attacks and guarantee that their activities continue by implementing comprehensive cybersecurity measures. Because disruptions in vital infrastructure sectors like electricity, healthcare, and transportation can have far-reaching effects, resilience is incredibly crucial.

Cybersecurity is crucial for regulatory compliance, data protection, and sustaining operations. Globally, regulatory agencies and governments have passed strict data protection legislation requiring businesses to have robust cybersecurity defenses. Severe penalties, legal ramifications, and reputational harm to a company are all possible outcomes of non-compliance. Organizations can avoid legal problems and show their dedication to safeguarding the privacy and data of their stakeholders by following these rules and guidelines.

Data and privacy protection is only one aspect of cybersecurity's importance in preserving national security. Cybercriminals and nation-states frequently attack defense systems, critical infrastructure, and government organizations to compromise national security operations and obtain sensitive data. Strong cybersecurity measures are necessary to counter these dangers and guarantee that infrastructure and data related to national security are shielded from cyberattacks and espionage. To create robust cyber defenses and protect national interests, governments must invest in cutting-edge cybersecurity technologies and work with partners in the private sector.

Furthermore, the promise of a safe online environment encompasses cybersecurity's broader societal effects. Strong cybersecurity is becoming necessary as digital technologies permeate more aspects of our daily lives, from wearables and smart homes to driverless cars and smart cities. Maintaining public safety, stopping cybercrime, and safeguarding individual privacy depends on secure technologies. To encourage digital inclusion and fairness, cybersecurity is also essential since safe online spaces allow more individuals to use online services and engage in the digital economy without worrying about security breaches.

A secure cyber environment must have both awareness and education as essential elements. We can build a more resilient digital society by teaching people and businesses the value of cybersecurity and arming them with the information and resources they need to stay safe. By enabling people to identify and successfully respond to cyber threats, cybersecurity awareness programs, training, and best practices can lower the overall risk of cyberattacks. Building a secure digital future requires promoting a mindset of proactive defense and cybersecurity awareness.

In conclusion, the significant advantages that strong cybersecurity offers to people, businesses, and society represent the promise of a secure cyber environment. Cybersecurity is essential to how the digital world works, from safeguarding private information and sensitive data to building trust, preserving business continuity, and adhering to legal obligations. We can create a resilient cyber environment that allows us to enjoy the advantages of digital technology while protecting our data, privacy, and national security by investing in cutting-edge cybersecurity measures, encouraging education and awareness, and fostering collaboration between the public and private sectors.

CHAPTER II

The Fundamentals of Cybersecurity

Key Concepts and Terminology

Anyone interested in securing digital assets and information must comprehend important ideas and terminology in the increasingly complicated world of cybersecurity. The CIA triad—confidentiality, integrity, and availability—are the cornerstones of cybersecurity and are essential to understanding. These guidelines offer a fundamental structure for assessing and putting security measures into place.

The goal of the confidentiality principle is to guarantee that information is only available to those permitted access. This entails safeguarding information from unwanted access and disclosure. Secure user authentication techniques, access control lists, and encryption are ways to guarantee confidentiality. Encryption protects data, even if intercepted during transmission, by converting it into a coded format that can only be decoded by an individual with the correct key. While authentication confirms a user's identity, access controls limit who can view or use resources. Retaining secrecy is essential to preventing unauthorized parties from accessing sensitive information, including financial records, personal data, and proprietary business information.

The second tenet of the CIA trinity, integrity, deals with the honesty and authenticity of information. It makes sure that no illegal changes have been made to the data. Integrity is when information is unaltered from source to destination, and systems do their intended tasks without unauthorized alteration. It encompasses both data and system integrity. Integrity-preserving methods include digital signatures, hashing, and checksums. Digital signatures confirm the integrity and authenticity of a message, software, or digital document, while checksums and hashing guarantee that data has not been altered. Maintaining data integrity is essential for preserving user confidence, particularly in sensitive systems like financial transactions and medical records where data correctness is crucial.

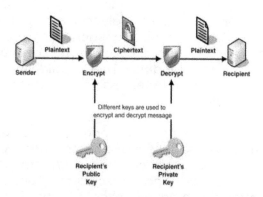

The idea of availability guarantees that resources and information are available to authorized users when needed. This entails ensuring the systems are functional and capable of responding to requests quickly. Regular maintenance, failover strategies, and redundancy are used to maintain availability. While failover mechanisms seamlessly transition to a backup system in the event of a primary system failure, redundancy entails having backup systems that can take over in such a scenario. By patching holes and keeping systems updated, routine maintenance helps avoid system breakdowns. Availability is essential for avoiding downtime and guaranteeing that services continue functioning, especially in vital industries like government, healthcare, and banking.

It is essential to comprehend key cybersecurity terminology in addition to the CIA trinity. One such word is "threat," which describes any possible risk to systems or information. There are many types of threats, such as malevolent actors like hackers, calamities caused by nature, or mistakes made by people. Another word for this is "vulnerability," which describes a system's flaw that a threat could use to obtain information without authorization or interfere with operations. One of the most critical aspects of cybersecurity is locating and fixing vulnerabilities.

An additional crucial phrase in cybersecurity is "risk." It symbolizes the risk of loss or harm if a threat takes advantage of a weakness. Identification and assessment of risks are necessary to ascertain their possible significance and probability. Using this assessment, companies can more efficiently deploy resources and prioritize security activities to address the most significant risks.

The term "attack vector" describes an attacker's route or technique to enter a system without authorization. Malware, social engineering, and phishing are common attack vectors. Creating defense strategies against attack vectors is facilitated by an understanding of them. For example, robust email filtering systems and user education can help reduce the impact of phishing, a tactic used by attackers to fool people into disclosing critical information.

The term "mitigation" describes the actions used to lessen the probability or severity of a cybersecurity event. Putting security measures in place, carrying out frequent security audits, and creating incident response plans are a few examples of mitigation techniques. These tactics seek to guarantee a speedy recovery and lessen the effects of security events.

The process of locating, handling, and getting over a cybersecurity event is known as "incidence response." When an event happens, an efficient incident response plan describes what to do. These actions include locating the incident, containing the threat, eliminating the cause, recovering from the incident, and evaluating the response to enhance future attempts. Reducing damage and returning to business as usual as soon as feasible depends on having a well-defined incident response plan.

A "zero-day vulnerability" is a software vulnerability unknown to the vendor of the targeted software, among other people who should be concerned about mitigating the risk. Zero-day vulnerabilities are severe because no patches or remedies are currently available, and they are unknown. Proactive security procedures and improved threat detection are necessary for detecting and mitigating zero-day vulnerabilities.

"Encryption," the technique of transforming data into a code to prevent unwanted access, is another essential idea. Encryption is frequently used in communication security, sensitive information protection, and data integrity verification. It is necessary to maintain confidentiality. Symmetric encryption, which utilizes a single key for both encryption and decryption and asymmetric encryption, which uses two keys—a public key and a private key—are the two main types of encryption.

A network security device known as a "firewall" monitors and regulates incoming and outgoing network traffic by pre-established security standards. As an essential part of network security, firewalls serve as a barrier between trusted and untrusted networks and prevent unwanted access.

Anyone working in the cybersecurity field has to be familiar with these foundational words and ideas. The CIA triad provides a fundamental framework for assessing and putting security measures into place, which stands for Confidentiality, Integrity, and Availability. This ensures that data is safe from unwanted access, is accurate and complete, and is accessible to authorized users when needed. Individuals and organizations may better safeguard their digital assets and traverse the challenging field of cybersecurity by understanding some fundamental concepts and vocabulary.

The Cybersecurity Framework

In a time when cyberattacks are common and getting more complex, a systematic approach to cybersecurity is crucial. The National Institute of Standards and Technology (NIST) created the Cybersecurity Framework, one of the most commonly used and acknowledged worldwide. It offers a thorough, risk-based method of managing cybersecurity that works for businesses of all sizes and industries. Furthermore, various international frameworks and standards are essential for defining best practices and directing global cybersecurity initiatives.

In 2014, in response to an executive order to enhance critical infrastructure cybersecurity in the United States, the NIST Cybersecurity Framework (CSF) was initially presented. The framework offers a collection of industry best practices and standards to enterprises so they may manage and lower cybersecurity risks. Because of its adaptability and flexibility, the NIST CSF can be tailored by businesses to meet their unique requirements and risk profiles.

Five high-level functions—Identify, Protect, Detect, Respond, and Recover—are the foundation of the NIST CSF. These roles offer a strategic perspective on how a company manages cybersecurity risk.

Understanding the corporate environment, the resources that enable essential operations, and the associated cybersecurity risks are all part of the "Identify" role. This covers risk assessment, risk management strategy, asset management, and governance. Organizations can more efficiently deploy resources and prioritize activities when these components are identified.

Putting safety measures in place to guarantee the provision of vital infrastructure services is the primary goal of the "Protect" function. It comprises maintenance, protective technology, data security, awareness and training, access control, and information protection processes and procedures. The prevention of cybersecurity incidents depends on this function.

Creating and executing actions to detect the presence of a cybersecurity event is part of the "Detect" function. Organizations can rapidly discover possible security incidents with continuous monitoring and detection mechanisms, facilitating prompt response and mitigation. The "Respond" function entails creating and carrying out plans to address a cybersecurity incident that has been recognized. Planning for responses, communicating, analyzing, mitigating, and improving are all part of this. Reaction plans that work are essential for reducing the damage caused by cybersecurity events.

Upholding resilience plans and restoring any services or capabilities compromised by a cybersecurity incident are part of the "Recover" role. Critical tasks in this function include communications, enhancements, and recovery planning. Ensuring that companies can promptly resume regular activities after an incident is the aim.

Other significant cybersecurity frameworks and standards are used worldwide besides the NIST CSF. The ISO/IEC 27001 standard, which outlines guidelines for creating, putting into practice, maintaining, and continuously enhancing an information security management system (ISMS), is one example of such a framework. The ISO/IEC 27001 standard offers a systematic approach to safeguarding confidential enterprise data. By using a risk management procedure, it addresses people, methods, and IT systems.

Based on a risk management methodology, the ISO/IEC 27001 framework specifies requirements for identifying, evaluating, and managing information security risks that are specific to the needs of the company. Additionally, it highlights how crucial it is to keep improving and regularly assess the ISMS to handle evolving threats and vulnerabilities.

The Payment Card Industry Data Security Standard (PCI DSS), which aims to safeguard cardholder data and secure credit card transactions, is another critical framework. A collection of security guidelines known as American Express, MasterCard, Visa, and other large credit card firms created PCI DSS. To safeguard cardholder data, it offers a baseline of technological and operational requirements. Organizations that process credit card payments must comply with PCI DSS, which lowers the risk of fraud and data breaches.

The European Union Agency for Cybersecurity (ENISA) also offers several frameworks and guidelines to improve cybersecurity throughout Europe. The General Data Protection Policy (GDPR), which places strict data protection obligations on companies managing the personal data of EU individuals, is one noteworthy policy. GDPR incorporates critical cybersecurity criteria, such as deploying suitable organizational and technical measures to maintain security proportional to the risk, even if its primary focus is data protection.

Another helpful framework is offered by the Center for Internet Security (CIS), called the CIS Controls. The most popular cyberattacks on systems and networks are lessened by the CIS Controls, a prioritized collection of best practices that provide defense-in-depth measures. These controls, widely acknowledged as valuable tools for enhancing cybersecurity posture, are created by a global community of cybersecurity specialists.

While these frameworks and standards have advantages and areas of emphasis, they all aim to manage cybersecurity risks, safeguard information assets, and make businesses resilient to cyberattacks. While the NIST CSF is especially well-suited for critical infrastructure and is extensively utilized in the US, other frameworks, such as ISO/IEC 27001 and PCI DSS, are used globally and provide thorough guidance for various elements of information security.

There are many advantages to putting a cybersecurity framework into practice. It assists businesses in recognizing and methodically managing cybersecurity threats, guaranteeing the safety of vital resources and data. It also makes it easier to comply with industry standards and regulatory obligations, which lowers the possibility of facing financial and legal repercussions. A well-known cybersecurity strategy can improve a company's standing and foster confidence among stakeholders, partners, and clients.

The NIST Cybersecurity Framework offers crucial guidance for controlling cybersecurity risks and safeguarding information assets, as do other international standards and frameworks, including ISO/IEC 27001, PCI DSS, GDPR, and CIS Controls. By providing an organized method for putting into practice strong cybersecurity measures, these frameworks help businesses protect their digital environments and effectively counteract online attacks. Organizations can strengthen their cybersecurity strategy, adhere to regulations, and create a safe base for their digital operations by implementing and incorporating these frameworks.

Risk Management in Cybersecurity

Risk management is essential to safeguarding information systems and digital assets in cybersecurity. The growing dependence of enterprises on technology has drastically increased the possibility of cyber threats, underscoring the need for sound risk management. This procedure entails locating, evaluating, and reducing threats to guarantee information security and integrity. Risk mitigation techniques are essential for lowering susceptibilities and preventing cyberattacks.

The identification of potential threats is the initial stage in cybersecurity risk management. This entails identifying the many hazards that could jeopardize a company's information systems. These risks come from inside threats, from irate workers to external cyber-attacks. Risks can also result from calamities caused by nature, technology, or incompetent people. A detailed awareness of the organization's assets, including its data, employees, hardware, and software, is necessary for a risk identification approach that is comprehensive. Organizations can better understand where they are most vulnerable by charting these assets and any possible weaknesses.

Assessing hazards comes next after they have been recognized. Evaluating each detected threat's likelihood and possible effects on the organization are critical components of risk assessment. Based on their seriousness and degree of hazard, this appraisal ranks risks in order of importance. This procedure can use various methodologies, such as hybrid, quantitative, and qualitative approaches. While quantitative assessments estimate risk using numerical data and statistical models, qualitative assessments rely on expert judgment and subjective analysis. Hybrid methods incorporate aspects of to offer a more impartial assessment. Sufficient risk evaluation necessitates ongoing observation and revision accommodate novel hazards and modifications in the establishment's surroundings.

Once risks have been identified and evaluated, the emphasis switches to creating plans for risk reduction. Putting policies in place to lessen the possibility and impact of possible hazards is known as risk mitigation. Risk avoidance is a popular tactic involving removing procedures or activities that might result in security breaches. For instance, a company may choose not to use a piece of software known to have security flaws. Reducing risk entails taking action to lessen the possible harm from a cyberattack. Implementing security technologies like intrusion detection systems, firewalls, and encryption can be one way to do this.

Transferring risks is another powerful mitigation tactic. By doing things like getting cyber insurance or contracting out specific tasks to a managed security service provider (MSSP), you can transfer the risk to a third party. Organizations may reduce their exposure to cyber dangers and ensure they have the resources to respond to incidents quickly by shifting risk. Nonetheless, it's critical to thoroughly assess outside suppliers to ensure they have robust security protocols.

Risk acceptance is the appropriate course of action when the expense of risk mitigation exceeds the potential consequences of the danger. In these situations, a company may accept the risk and take little to no action to mitigate it. This strategy is frequently employed when dealing with low-impact threats that wouldn't seriously impair operations. Nonetheless, companies must record and explain to interested parties the reasoning behind taking on such risks.

A robust incident response strategy must be created and implemented for risk mitigation. The actions to be performed in the case of a cyberattack are outlined in this plan, along with roles and duties, communication guidelines, and recovery techniques. By regularly testing and updating the incident response plan, the company may minimize damage and expedite recovery by being ready to respond to security occurrences quickly and effectively.

It's also critical to cultivate a security-aware culture within the company. Programs for employee education and training can lower the possibility of human error by assisting staff in identifying and addressing possible dangers. Simple yet efficient ways to improve security include implementing robust access controls and changing passwords regularly.

To sum up, risk management in cybersecurity is a complex process that entails locating, evaluating, and reducing risks to safeguard a company's digital assets. Through comprehension of possible hazards and execution of suitable tactics, establishments can considerably diminish their susceptibility to cyber assaults. Maintaining a culture of security awareness, updating risk assessments regularly, and engaging in continuous monitoring are all essential components of effective risk management. Cyber threat strategies and countermeasures must also adapt and change with time to keep enterprises resilient in the face of a constantly shifting threat landscape.

Building a Cybersecurity Culture

Given the constant presence and sophistication of cyber threats in today's digital environment, organizations must establish a strong cybersecurity culture. At all organizational levels, a cybersecurity culture prioritizes security, ensuring staff members are informed about potential risks and prepared to take appropriate action. The importance of awareness and training in establishing this culture cannot be emphasized, as they are crucial to developing a security-first mindset that penetrates the whole business.

The cornerstone of a cybersecurity culture is awareness. Workers need to be aware of several cyber threats, such as malware, ransomware, phishing scams, and social engineering techniques. Employees are more susceptible to these risks if they are unaware of them, which could jeopardize the company's security. Raising awareness entails teaching staff members about the dangers and arming them with the information they need to identify and steer clear of any threats. Since cyber hazards are constantly changing and staff need to stay up to date on the newest strategies employed by cybercriminals, this education should be ongoing.

Training enhances awareness by giving staff members the knowledge and resources they need to defend the company against online dangers. Many subjects are covered in practical training programs, such as how to spot phishing emails, handle sensitive data securely, and communicate via secure channels. Exercises involving hands-on learning, like phishing simulations, can be very useful in consolidating knowledge and ensuring staff members are equipped to react effectively in practical situations. Businesses may guarantee that their staff members remain watchful and proactive regarding cybersecurity by incorporating training into routine processes and establishing it as a fundamental component of the corporate culture.

More than awareness and training are needed to foster a security-first mindset; security must be ingrained in the organization's fundamental processes and values. A critical part of this process is leadership. Executives and managers may set a strong example for staff members at all levels by prioritizing cybersecurity and exhibiting a dedication to safeguarding the company's digital assets. Leaders should constantly explain cybersecurity's importance, underscoring its relevance to the organization's overall performance and resilience. Leaders may foster a culture where security is viewed as everyone's responsibility by incorporating cybersecurity into the organization's mission and goals.

Developing a cybersecurity culture requires leadership support and the application of best practices that promote safe behaviors and emphasize the value of security. Creating detailed, comprehensive security policies is one such procedure. These guidelines should include data protection procedures, approved technology use, and reporting and response procedures for security incidents. Organizations can guarantee that everyone knows their part in ensuring security and the actions they must take to safeguard the company by giving staff clear rules.

One such recommended approach is to promote candid dialogue around cybersecurity. Workers should not be afraid to report possible security flaws or vulnerabilities for fear of retaliation. Establishing a space where workers feel comfortable asking questions and sharing their worries promotes a feeling of group accountability. It aids in seeing possible risks before they get out of hand. Employees can discuss cybersecurity issues and best practices by participating in regularly scheduled security forums and meetings.

Organizations should allocate resources toward appropriate technology and equipment to aid their cybersecurity endeavors. Implementing advanced security solutions, such as firewalls, intrusion detection systems, and encryption, can assist protect the organization's digital assets. However, more than technology is needed; appropriate training must be provided to guarantee that staff members can utilize these instruments efficiently. Organizations should also regularly upgrade their security protocols to avoid emerging threats and maintain strong defenses.

Another essential component of creating a cybersecurity culture is continuous improvement. Businesses should evaluate their cybersecurity procedures regularly, pinpoint areas for development, and make necessary adjustments. This may entail carrying out routine security audits, evaluating incident response plans, and getting input from staff members regarding the efficacy of training initiatives. Through proactive cybersecurity measures, organizations can maintain an advantage over future threats and bolster their defenses over time.

To sum up, creating a cybersecurity culture is a complex process that calls for a dedication to best practices, training, and awareness. Employers may equip their staff to identify and successfully address cyber threats by encouraging a security-first mentality. A robust cybersecurity culture must have open communication, transparent policies, strong leadership, and a commitment to ongoing improvement. Organizations must be proactive and alert to safeguard their digital assets as cyber threats change, making security a fundamental component of their corporate identity.

CHAPTER III

Cyber Threat Landscape

Common Cyber Threats and Attack Vectors

Cyber-attacks are a recurring and expanding worry for individuals and organizations in the digital era. Creating effective defenses requires an understanding of these threats' characteristics and the assault routes they use. Malware, viruses, and worms are among the most frequent cyber threats, phishing, and social engineering scams. These dangers can do significant damage, from financial loss and data breaches to service interruption and trust erosion.

Malicious software such as viruses, worms, and malware are created to infect, harm to infect, harm, or take down machines and networks. When a legitimate application or file is infected with malicious code, it can spread to other hosts when the infected program is run. This is known as a virus. Viruses can destroy data, remove files, and interfere with system operation once launched. Worms, however, are autonomously propagating programs that don't need a host file or human intervention to propagate. They spread quickly across networks, using bandwidth and delivering payloads that might damage computers by taking advantage of flaws in operating systems and network protocols.

Malware is a general phrase that includes a wide range of malicious software, such as trojans, spyware, ransomware, and viruses and worms. Spyware is made to secretly record and gather user data, including surfing patterns, personal information, and keystrokes. Ransomware causes significant disruption and monetary loss by encrypting the victim's data and demanding money for the decryption key. Trojan horses pose as safe software, but within, they are loaded with malicious code that can open backdoors, steal information, or enable more attacks.

Phishing is a type of social engineering in which someone is tricked into disclosing private information, including credit card numbers, usernames, and passwords. Misleading emails, texts, or websites from reliable sources are used to accomplish this. Phishing attempts frequently incite panic or a sense of urgency to make victims act quickly, like clicking on a dangerous link or downloading a corrupted attachment. Once the victim accepts the bait, the attacker can infect the victim's device with malware or obtain access to personal data.

Attacks using social engineering take advantage of human psychology instead of technological flaws. These attacks depend on coercing people into doing things or disclosing private information. Tailgating, baiting, and pretexting are common strategies. Pretexting is fabricating a situation to get information from the victim. An attacker might, for instance, pose as an IT support specialist and request login information to fix a made-up problem. Offering the victim something alluring, such as free software or a USB stick infected with malware, is known as baiting. Tailgating, also known as piggybacking, is the practice of an attacker evading physical security measures by trailing an authorized individual into a restricted area.

These cyber-threats can have disastrous effects. Identity theft, financial fraud, and reputational harm can arise from data breaches that lead to economic, intellectual property, and personal information loss. Businesses may incur significant costs due to system outages, data loss, and decreased productivity caused by infected systems. In addition, recovering after a cyberattack can take a long time and need a lot of resources. It involves restoring the system, improving security, and adhering to legal and regulatory requirements.

People and institutions must take a multi-layered security approach to protect themselves from these prevalent cyber threats. This entails installing technical safeguards like firewalls, intrusion detection systems, antivirus software, and encryption. Patch management and regular software updates are necessary to fix known vulnerabilities and stop attacks. Programs for user education and awareness are also essential since they enable people to identify social engineering and phishing attempts. Promoting excellent practices can drastically lower the likelihood of being a victim of cyberattacks. These practices include creating strong passwords, turning on multi-factor authentication, and avoiding dubious links and attachments.

It is recommended that organizations create and implement all-encompassing security policies that delineate protocols for handling and safeguarding confidential data. Regular penetration testing and security assessments can help find weaknesses and fortify defenses. Incident response plans must be created and routinely verified to guarantee a prompt and efficient response to any security breaches. An organization's capacity to identify and address new threats can be further improved by working with cybersecurity professionals and remaining current on the most recent threat intelligence.

In conclusion, some of the most prevalent and hazardous cyber threats available today are malware, worms, viruses, phishing, and social engineering schemes. Creating effective defenses requires understanding these threats' mechanisms and the possible harm they can do. By implementing solid technical controls, cultivating a security-conscious culture, and maintaining attentive monitoring and response protocols, individuals and organizations can effectively reduce the potential hazards associated with these ubiquitous cyber threats. Because cyber threats are constantly changing, cybersecurity must be approached with a proactive and flexible mindset to ensure defenses are strong even in the face of fresh dangers.

Advanced Persistent Threats (APTs)

A sophisticated and persistent cyberattack directed towards a particular target, usually a nation-state, business, or political group, is an advanced persistent threat, or APT. APTs differ from other types of cyber threats in that they covertly infiltrate the victim's network and remain there for a considerable amount of time, gathering information or causing damage. APTs' main objectives are to permanently take over a target's systems, disrupt operations, or steal confidential data.

APTs can be distinguished from other kinds of cyber threats by their features. One of their distinguishing characteristics is their advanced nature, which uses a mix of unique malware, zero-day exploits, and cunning social engineering techniques to penetrate and hold onto a target network. These attacks are carefully prepared and carried out by highly competent attackers, who frequently have access to significant resources. Because of their sophistication, APTs are challenging to identify and counter using conventional security methods.

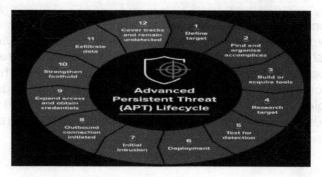

Another essential feature of APTs is persistence. Attackers create a footing and use various strategies to stay active after getting access to a network. This can involve installing rootkits to conceal their actions from security monitoring tools, constructing backdoors, and moving laterally within the network using authentic credentials. Because they can stay hidden for extended periods, attackers can accomplish their goals without informing the victim.

APTs' targeted nature is also essential. Attacks with a targeted intent, or APTs, differ from opportunistic ones that spread widely. The targets are picked based on their strategic importance, such as if they hold secret military, diplomatic, or economic knowledge. This focused strategy entails an in-depth survey to comprehend the target's personnel, security protocols, and network architecture. Then, this knowledge creates customized attacks to increase the likelihood of success.

APTs can have serious consequences, including significant data breaches, intellectual property theft, monetary loss, and harm to national security. Because these attacks are so covert, the perpetrators may have accessed enormous volumes of data or done irreparable damage when detected.

Several noteworthy APT cases demonstrate the complexity and significance of these threats. Stuxnet, identified in 2010, is among the most notorious APTs. Stuxnet, a highly developed computer worm, was directed at Iran's nuclear program. It was intended to physically harm centrifuges used for uranium enrichment while staying undetected by operators. Many people think that Israel and the United States worked together to create Stuxnet, which marks a dramatic increase in the employment of cyberweapons for geopolitical objectives.

APT29, also called Cozy Bear or The Dukes, is another noteworthy example. APT29 has operated since 2008 and is connected to the Russian government. This group is well-known for its espionage operations, which have targeted military, diplomatic, and political institutions worldwide. The 2016 breach of the Democratic National Committee (DNC) in the United States was one of their most well-known operations; it led to the loss and disclosure of private emails and changed the political landscape.

APT28 is another Russian-affiliated group that has a history of high-profile attacks. It is also known by the names Fancy Bear and Sofacy. APT28 has been in operation since the middle of the 2000s and targets media, governmental, and military institutions. Their 2015 attack on the German Bundestag, in which they broke into the legislative network, stole information, and interfered with communications, was one of their most prominent operations.

APT groups are also well-known in China, with APT1, commonly referred to as Comment Crew, being one of the best-documented. APT1 is thought to have conducted extensive cyber espionage operations targeting various industries, including aerospace, telecommunications, and energy. It has been connected to the Chinese military. The cybersecurity firm Mandiant exposed APT1's tactics and connected them to the Chinese government in a 2013 report that described the group's activities.

Organizations must implement a multi-layered security strategy incorporating incident response capabilities, continuous monitoring, and sophisticated threat detection to protect themselves from advanced persistent threats (APTs). Conventional security tools, such as firewalls and antivirus programs, frequently need to catch up against APT actors' advanced strategies. Advanced security solutions, such as intrusion detection systems (IDS), endpoint detection and response (EDR) tools, and security information and event management (SIEM) systems, should be implemented by enterprises instead. These tools can assist in identifying abnormal behaviors that point to the presence of an APT.

Organizations must invest in cybersecurity awareness, training programs, and technological measures to enable staff members to identify and counteract social engineering attacks. Frequent penetration tests and security audits help find weaknesses and bolster defenses against possible APT assaults.

Finally, it should be noted that advanced persistent threats pose a serious and intricate threat to cybersecurity. They are especially deadly because of their advanced, persistent, and targeted nature, which allows them to do significant harm before being discovered. APTs have substantial geopolitical ramifications, as demonstrated by notable cases like Stuxnet, APT29, and APT28, emphasizing the necessity of robust and multi-layered security plans. Organizations can better prepare and defend themselves against these dangers by knowing the traits and effects of advanced persistent threats (APTs).

Insider Threats

Organizations are at serious risk from insider threats because they involve employees with authorized access to confidential data and systems. These threats can be challenging to identify and neutralize because insiders frequently possess information and trust that external attackers do not share. Protecting organizational assets requires understanding insider threat kinds and motivations, as well as practical detection and mitigation techniques.

There are various forms of insider threats, and each poses different difficulties. The malevolent insider, who aims to cause deliberate damage to the organization, is one of the main kinds. This person might take part in actions like stealing private information, breaking into systems, or disclosing private data. Malevolent insiders may have a variety of motivations, such as monetary gain, retaliation, adherence to particular ideologies, or external compulsion. For example, workers who perceive mistreatment from their jobs may steal confidential data to resell to other companies or utilize it to launch their venture.

The careless insider is another kind of insider threat. In contrast to malevolent insiders, negligence insiders do not intentionally inflict harm; instead, their reckless activities unintentionally do so. This could be ignoring security procedures, falling for phishing scams, or improperly handling sensitive data. For instance, a worker may unintentionally send a private document to the incorrect person via email or utilize weak passwords that are simple to crack. Since careless insiders frequently don't realize the possible repercussions of their actions, education, and training are essential in combating this issue.

The compromised insider is the third category. The credentials or systems of these persons have been infiltrated by external attackers, who subsequently leverage the insider's access to gain access to the organization. This can happen in several ways, including social engineering, malware, and phishing. An insider who has been infiltrated may inadvertently download malicious software, giving attackers access to the network. Once entered, attackers can travel laterally, pretending to be authorized users while stealing data or causing havoc.

There are many different and intricate reasons why insider threats occur. Gaining money is a typical incentive, especially for insiders with bad intentions. Workers struggling financially or drawn in by attractive offers from other companies may sell trade secrets or embezzle money. Insider threats are also motivated by complaints or retaliation, as workers who feel undervalued or mistreated may want to damage the company. Additionally, ideological motivations may come into play, especially when political objectives or hacktivism are involved. Strongly religious workers may act against the interests of their company to further a cause or bring attention to perceived injustices.

Insider threat detection and prevention necessitate an all-encompassing strategy incorporating technology, regulations, and training. Putting in place reliable monitoring and logging systems is one efficient detection technique. These systems monitor user activity and report anomalous activity, such as downloading data or accessing sensitive files after hours. Organizations can spot anomalies pointing to insider threats more quickly by setting baselines for typical behavior. User and Entity Behavior Analytics (UEBA) technologies are beneficial as they employ machine learning to identify patterns and deviations that may indicate a threat.

Essential preventive measures include most minor privilege guidelines and access limits. Insider dangers can be minimized by limiting employee access to only the data and systems required for their job. If an insider does turn malevolent, the potential damage can be minimized, and unauthorized access can be prevented by routinely checking and changing access rights. Furthermore, multi-factor authentication (MFA) offers additional protection, making it more challenging for hacked credentials to be used fraudulently.

Programs for employee awareness and education are essential for reducing careless insider threats. The likelihood of unintentional breaches can be significantly decreased by regular training on cybersecurity best practices, such as identifying phishing efforts and treating sensitive information appropriately. Overall, organizational security depends on fostering a culture of security awareness among staff members, where they recognize the value of adhering to security procedures and feel empowered to report questionable activity.

Additionally, organizations must establish explicit policies and processes for dealing with insider risks. Part of this is a clear incident response plan specifying what to do if an insider threat is discovered. Routine drills and simulations can ensure staff preparedness for effective response. To discourage hostile behavior, it is essential to communicate the legal and disciplinary repercussions for violating security standards.

Another crucial tactic is to include insider threat programs that concentrate on locating and reducing such threats. To detect and counter insider threats, these programs frequently entail interdisciplinary teams comprising HR, legal, and IT specialists. Organizations can enhance their understanding of insider threats and devise more productive mitigation strategies by adopting a comprehensive approach.

In conclusion, insider threats pose a serious concern because insiders have access to information and knowledge. Developing successful detection and prevention techniques requires understanding the types and motivations of insider threats. Insiders who are malicious, careless, or compromised each present different hazards since their goals might range from monetary gain to retaliation or ideological convictions. Organizations can lessen these concerns by implementing robust monitoring systems, imposing stringent access controls, training staff members on cybersecurity best practices, and creating extensive insider threat programs. Organizations can more effectively defend themselves against insider threats, which are dynamic and complex, by implementing a proactive and multidimensional strategy.

Emerging Threats and Trends

Due to the quick development of technologies like artificial intelligence (AI), the Internet of Things (IoT), and other cutting-edge breakthroughs, the cybersecurity landscape is constantly changing. While these technologies have many advantages, companies must also be aware of their new dangers and vulnerabilities. Creating effective cybersecurity plans requires an understanding of the effects of these technologies as well as an ability to predict future trends.

The Internet of Things (IoT) has completely changed how gadgets communicate, resulting in a highly networked world where commonplace items, such as industrial gear and residential appliances, are online. IoT increases productivity and ease of use but also makes more space available for cyberattacks. Because many IoT devices lack robust security features, hackers can easily target them. The installation of sophisticated security measures is hampered by these devices' frequently low processing and memory capacities. IoT devices are also more vulnerable because they usually use default passwords and don't receive regular software updates.

Massive botnets, in which many hacked devices are utilized to launch coordinated attacks, pose a severe threat due to IoT. This potential was shown in the 2016 Mirai botnet assault, which used thousands of infected IoT devices to launch a massive Distributed Denial of Service (DDoS) attack that interfered with essential internet services. To stop similar large-scale attacks, the security of IoT devices and networks will become increasingly important as their number grows.

Machine learning (ML) and artificial intelligence (AI) are revolutionizing several industries, including cybersecurity. AI can improve defensive threat detection and response by sifting through enormous volumes of data to find trends and abnormalities that point to cyber threats. Security systems powered by AI can learn from and adapt to new threats, which gradually increases their efficacy. AI, for example, can be used to identify and stop phishing attempts by identifying questionable content and examining email trends.

However, when applied by malevolent parties, AI also poses serious threats. Attackers can use AI to create more intricate and focused attacks. Attacks can be carried out more quickly and extensively using AI to automate finding vulnerabilities and developing exploits. AI-driven deepfake technology presents an additional growing hazard by producing audio and video content that appears natural but is fraudulent. Deepfakes can be employed in social engineering assaults, disinformation operations, and even extortion.

These hazards are increased by the confluence of AI and IoT, sometimes known as the AIoT (Artificial Intelligence of Things). If not adequately secured, AIoT systems—which employ AI to manage and optimize IoT devices—can be especially vulnerable. Attackers may be able to control many IoT devices by compromising an AIoT system, which could lead to extensive disruption.

Known for its part in cryptocurrency, blockchain technology is also changing cybersecurity. Blockchain is a potential technology for improving security and privacy since it is decentralized and unchangeable. It can be applied to guarantee data integrity, secure transactions, and identity verification. Blockchain technology is not impervious to attacks, though. Self-executing contracts, known as "smart contracts," in which the terms are encoded directly into the code, may have flaws that hackers might exploit. Furthermore, blockchain's anonymity can make illicit activity easier, like paying for ransomware.

Future threats are expected to be shaped by several developments. The Internet of Things will expand even quicker because of the growing use of 5G technology, providing faster and more dependable internet connections. But 5G networks' faster speeds and lower latency may also make it possible for more advanced cyberattacks. Network security is more challenging because 5G infrastructure is dispersed and depends on many small cell towers.

Another emerging technology that has enormous cybersecurity implications is quantum computing. When quantum computers are developed to their full potential, they can crack even the most sophisticated encryption methods. This might make current encryption approaches outdated and call for creating quantum-resistant cryptographic technologies. Staying ahead of this curve will be necessary for organizations to safeguard their confidential information from possible quantum threats.

Cybersecurity strategies have to change to meet these new threats. To detect and respond to threats, organizations must take a more proactive and flexible approach to security, utilizing cutting-edge technology like artificial intelligence and machine learning. For threats to be identified and mitigated before they do significant harm, ongoing monitoring and real-time threat intelligence will be essential. Furthermore, an emphasis on safeguarding the whole supply chain—including independent contractors and Internet of Things devices—will be crucial to handle the increased attack surface.

Corporations, governments, and cybersecurity specialists must collaborate and share information to combat evolving threats. A more cohesive defense against skilled cyber adversaries can be achieved by exchanging threat knowledge and best practices. Moreover, to ensure that security precautions keep up with technical developments, regulatory frameworks and standards must change to meet the particular difficulties presented by developing technologies.

In conclusion, there are many different ways that new technologies like blockchain, AI, and the Internet of Things are changing cybersecurity. Although there are many advantages to modern technologies, they also bring new dangers and weaknesses, necessitating creative and flexible security solutions. The development of quantum computing and the deployment of 5G are two future phenomena that will significantly alter the security landscape. Organizations may enhance their security and safeguard their digital assets in a world that is becoming more linked by comprehending these new risks and keeping up with technical developments.

CHAPTER IV

Cybersecurity Prevention Strategies

Network Security Measures

Network security is a top business priority in today's digitally connected world. To defend against cyber-attacks, data integrity, confidentiality, and availability must be protected while it moves across networks. Firewalls, virtual private networks (VPNs), intrusion detection and prevention systems (IDPS), and secure network topologies are some of the most critical security tools. Each of these elements is essential to building a solid defense against malicious activity and guaranteeing efficient and safe use of network resources.

One of the most essential components of network security is a firewall. Monitoring and regulating incoming and outgoing network traffic by preset security criteria is a barrier between an internal network and external sources, such as the Internet. Software-based, hardware-based, or a combination of both can be firewalls. Depending on protocols, IP addresses, and port numbers, they review data packets and decide whether they should be banned or permitted. Firewalls shield networks from various threats, such as viruses, worms, and unauthorized users, by filtering traffic to prevent unwanted access.

Network security is enhanced by intrusion detection and prevention systems (IDPS), which monitor network traffic for unusual activity and take proactive steps to stop possible breaches. An intrusion detection system (IDS) looks for deviations from the norm in network traffic patterns to identify unusual activity and potential security breaches. An IDS notifies administrators when it finds a potential threat so they can look into it and take the necessary action. An intrusion prevention system (IPS) goes above and beyond simple detection by actively thwarting identified threats. An IPS can react to possible threats faster by automatically blocking or quarantining harmful traffic in real time. By reducing the impact of security incidents, IDS and IPS work together to help organizations detect and respond to threats more effectively.

Another essential element of network security is virtual private networks, or VPNs, particularly in this day and age of widespread remote work and mobile access. Over a less secure network, like the Internet, a VPN establishes a secure, encrypted connection. This guarantees the privacy and security of any data transferred between the user and the organization's network. VPNs are necessary for safeguarding private data against interception and eavesdropping, mainly when staff members use public Wi-Fi hotspots or other unsafe areas to access the network. VPNs contribute to the secrecy and integrity of communications by encrypting data flow, making it much more difficult for hackers to exploit weaknesses.

Building a solid defense against cyberattacks requires secure network topologies. A well-thought-out network architecture uses the defense-in-depth principle and several tiers of security measures. This strategy ensures that even in the event of a breach in one layer of security, other layers will still provide protection. Segmentation, which divides the network into smaller, isolated segments to restrict the spread of viruses and illegal access, is one of the critical elements of a secure network architecture. Thanks to network segmentation, organizations can apply more stringent access rules and monitor traffic inside each section more effectively.

Robust access control mechanisms are a crucial component of a secure network architecture. This involves confirming the identities of people and devices gaining access to the network through authentication techniques like multi-factor authentication (MFA). By requiring users to submit two or more means of verification, like a password and a fingerprint, MFA increases the difficulty of unwanted access by attackers. Furthermore, role-based access control (RBAC) minimizes the possibility of insider threats. It lowers the attack surface by guaranteeing that users can only access the resources required for their responsibilities.

A secure network architecture also requires vulnerability management and routine network monitoring. Organizations may quickly identify and address abnormalities and possible security incidents using continuous monitoring. The vulnerability management process is routinely checking the network for security flaws and implementing updates and fixes to address vulnerabilities. By proactively identifying and remedying security weaknesses, companies can lower the likelihood of successful attacks.

Moreover, network communication security is greatly aided by encryption. Data encryption ensures that even in the unlikely event that an attacker intercepts it, they cannot read it without the decryption key. Sensitive data, including financial and personal information as well as intellectual property, is further protected by this.

Apart from the aforementioned technical steps, cultivating a security-aware culture within the firm is vital. Best practices for network security, such as identifying phishing attempts, creating strong passwords, and reporting suspicious activity, should be taught to staff members. Employee empowerment and education as the first line of defense is essential because human error plays a significant role in many security breaches.

To sum up, to safeguard enterprises from various cyber threats, network security solutions like firewalls, intrusion detection and prevention systems, VPNs, and secure network topologies are crucial. By filtering traffic, firewalls act as the initial line of protection, and IDPS offers more sophisticated monitoring and response capabilities. To guard against internal and external threats, secure network architectures have numerous layers of security, in addition to VPNs, guaranteeing secure communications over untrusted networks. Organizations can significantly improve their capacity to safeguard confidential data and uphold the availability and integrity of their network resources by putting these precautions into practice and encouraging a culture of security awareness. Maintaining vigilance and proactivity in protecting network infrastructures will continue to be a top responsibility for businesses globally as cyber threats advance.

Endpoint Security

In cybersecurity initiatives, endpoint security has grown in importance for businesses of all sizes. Protecting individual devices and endpoints is crucial to securing the more extensive network due to the increase in mobile devices, laptops, and remote work. Endpoint security protects all connected devices, including laptops, desktop computers, cell phones, and other gadgets, against attacks that can jeopardize the network. Antivirus and anti-malware programs are essential components of endpoint protection, which are made to identify, stop, and handle different kinds of dangerous software and online threats.

In an organization's network, endpoints are among the weakest links. Endpoint security is critical since every endpoint might be a possible entry point for hackers. The growing trend of "Bring Your Device" (BYOD), or using personal devices for work functions, makes the security environment more challenging. These individual devices are more vulnerable to assaults because they might not follow the same security guidelines as hardware provided by the enterprise. Ensuring every endpoint is secure contributes to preserving the network's integrity and guarding against security breaches involving sensitive data.

Antivirus software is one of the earliest and most popular types of endpoint protection. They look for known viruses and other harmful software in files and programs. A collection of virus signatures—unique data strings that identify particular kinds of malware—is the foundation of antivirus software. The antivirus software marks a file or program as harmful and takes the necessary action, such as quarantining or deleting it when the signature in the database matches the file. Conventional antivirus programs work well against known threats but could have trouble identifying novel, unidentified malware variations. As a result, heuristic analysis is a common feature of contemporary antivirus software, enabling it to detect questionable activity even in the absence of a particular signature in the database.

Anti-malware solutions cover a broader spectrum of threats by going beyond the capabilities of typical antivirus software. Malware, an acronym for harmful software, comprises ransomware, spyware, worms, trojans, viruses, and adware. Anti-malware programs employ various detection methods to find and neutralize these threats, including behavioral analysis, machine learning, and signature-based detection. Using behavioral analysis to identify any odd or potentially dangerous activity, software behavior is observed. For instance, an indication of ransomware activity may be a program's attempt to encrypt a lot of data, in which case the anti-malware program would step in.

The efficiency of antivirus and anti-malware programs has been dramatically increased by the incorporation of machine learning and artificial intelligence (AI). Large volumes of data may be analyzed using machine learning algorithms, which can then be used to spot trends and abnormalities linked to harmful activity. By constantly absorbing fresh information, these algorithms become more adept at identifying and neutralizing new threats. The time it takes to contain and eliminate assaults can be decreased using AI-driven security solutions, which can help automate reactions to discovered threats. This is especially crucial when dealing with complex, swiftly spreading threats that might spread quickly throughout a network.

Endpoint Detection and Response (EDR) systems represent a sophisticated method of endpoint security. Real-time monitoring and analysis of endpoint actions is made possible by EDR solutions, which help enterprises identify and address threats more successfully. To spot suspicious activity, such as unexpected network connections, unauthorized access attempts, or unusual file alterations, EDR solutions gather and analyze data from endpoints. EDR tools can isolate impacted endpoints, stop malicious activity, and start remediation procedures when a threat is identified. Security teams may develop more effective response and preventive measures by better understanding the nature and breadth of an attack with the assistance of comprehensive forensic information.

Even with the improvements in antivirus and anti-malware software, endpoint security is still complex. Attackers are always coming up with new ways to get around security systems, which means cyber risks constantly change. Using malware that is polymorphic— that is, continuously modifying its code to avoid being detected by antivirus programs that rely on signatures—is one such tactic. The growing ubiquity of fileless malware, which lives in memory rather than on the hard drive and is more difficult to find with conventional scanning techniques, presents another difficulty. To tackle these obstacles, entities must embrace a tiered strategy for safeguarding endpoints, integrating several defensive mechanisms to establish an all-encompassing security stance.

Adequate endpoint security also requires user awareness and training. Social engineering and phishing are two examples of cyberattacks that directly target users. Employee education about typical dangers and how to avoid them can drastically lower the likelihood that an assault will be effective. Training courses, for instance, can instruct users on spot phishing emails, steer clear of dubious links, and report any strange activity. Organizations can improve their security posture and lower the risk of endpoint intrusions by cultivating a security-conscious culture.

To summarize, endpoint security is essential to safeguarding corporate networks and data. Antivirus and anti-malware programs are crucial to this endeavor since they protect against various online dangers. These solutions are now much more effective due to the incorporation of cutting-edge technologies like AI and machine learning. Nonetheless, a comprehensive strategy for endpoint security that includes EDR solutions, user awareness, and ongoing monitoring is necessary due to the dynamic nature of the threat landscape. Organizations may enhance their ability to fend against cyberattacks on their endpoints and, consequently, their entire network by implementing robust endpoint security measures. Ensuring strong endpoint security will continue to be a global primary concern for enterprises as cyber-attacks escalate in sophistication and complexity.

Data Protection Techniques

Data protection is a significant concern for all types of enterprises in the modern digital era. Data breaches and unauthorized access are always risky because of the growing volume of private data being moved and stored electronically. A thorough data security plan must include secure data storage and transmission procedures and data protection mechanisms like encryption and data masking. These methods guarantee that private data stays undamaged, private, and accessible to authorized parties only.

One of the best ways to protect data is with encryption. It entails transforming text data from plain form into ciphertext, a coded format that can only be cracked by an individual with the correct decryption key. This procedure ensures that data stays unreadable and inoperable for unauthorized users, even if it is intercepted or viewed without authorization. Symmetric and asymmetric encryption are the two main categories of encryption. The same key is used in symmetric encryption for both encryption and decryption. This technique works well for encrypting significant volumes of data since it is quick and effective. The difficulty, though, is in safely transferring the encryption key between participants.

In contrast, asymmetric encryption employs a set of two keys: a private key for decryption and a public key for encryption. Although this approach can be slower and require more processing power, it offers greater security for key distribution. Through the use of hybrid encryption, which combines the two methods, businesses can take use of each technique's advantages.

Another essential method for safeguarding sensitive data is data masking. Protecting sensitive information while maintaining the dataset's usefulness for analysis and testing entails hiding some data. Several techniques can hide data, including encryption, shuffling, and substitution. Substitution replaces sensitive data with plausible but fake data to keep the masked data operational for testing. Data within the dataset is shuffled to preserve its integrity while masking the original values.

Sensitive information can also be hidden using encryption; however, doing so requires decrypting the data, which poses a danger to security if improperly handled.

One essential component of data safety is secure data storage. It entails implementing policies to guarantee that data is protected from loss, corruption, and unwanted access. Encryption is one of the main techniques for safe data storage. Organizations can safeguard confidential data on servers, databases, and other storage devices by encrypting the data at rest. Secure data storage also requires access controls. Ensuring that only authorized individuals can access sensitive data is ensured by putting robust authentication techniques, such as multi-factor authentication (MFA), into place. Furthermore, role-based access control (RBAC) reduces the possibility of insider threats by limiting access to data according to a user's job inside the company.

Another crucial element of safe data storage is routine data backups. Backups give important data a safety net by guaranteeing that it can be recovered in the case of a loss or corruption. To guard against outside dangers like fire or theft, backups should be kept in a safe, off-site location. Another essential procedure is to test backups to ensure they can be restored regularly.

Both secure storage and secure data transit are crucial. Data is frequently sent over networks, such as the internet, where nefarious individuals may intercept it. To secure data while it is in transit, encryption is essential. Secure Sockets Layer (SSL) and Transport Layer Security (TLS) are two popular techniques for encrypting data sent over the internet. As information moves between the sender and the recipient, these protocols guarantee that it stays private and unaltered. VPNs, or virtual private networks, are another valuable instrument for safe data transit. With VPNs, data may move over a secure, encrypted tunnel that keeps it safe from eavesdropping and interception. This is especially crucial for remote employees who must access sensitive data from outside the company network.

To further guarantee that data is transferred securely, enterprises should implement secure file transfer protocols like Managed File Transfer (MFT) and Secure File Transfer Protocol (SFTP). These protocols provide increased security features like auditing, authentication, and encryption to safeguard data during transfer.

In conclusion, secure data storage and transit mechanisms and data protection strategies like encryption and data masking are crucial parts of an all-encompassing data security plan. Data confidentiality and security are guaranteed by encryption, even if unauthorized users intercept it. Sensitive information is protected by data masking, which also keeps valuable data for testing and analysis. Implementing safeguards like encryption, access limits, and routine backups is necessary for secure data storage to guard against loss, corruption, and unwanted access. To protect data while it is in transit, secure file transfer techniques, VPNs, and encryption protocols are used in safe data transfer. Organizations may preserve data integrity, secure sensitive information, and guarantee regulatory compliance by implementing these data protection strategies. Maintaining robust data protection procedures will always be crucial for businesses worldwide as cyber threats change.

Application Security

Application security is essential to shield software programs from flaws and ensure they are resilient against online attacks. It includes a range of procedures and techniques designed to keep apps safe across the whole development and implementation process. Regular software upgrades with efficient patch management and secure coding techniques are essential application security components.

Developing software that is resistant to malicious assaults and vulnerabilities requires the use of secure coding standards. It entails writing code that puts security first by adhering to industry-standard norms and concepts. Input validation, which ensures user inputs are verified and cleaned to stop injection attacks like SQL injection and cross-site scripting (XSS), is a central tenet of secure coding. Developers can lessen the possibility of an attacker introducing malicious code or commands into the program by verifying and cleaning inputs.

Implementing appropriate permission and authentication procedures is a crucial component of secure coding. While authorization decides what resources and actions users can access based on their roles and privileges, authentication confirms the identity of users gaining access to the program. To reduce the effect of possible security breaches, secure coding practices include using robust authentication techniques, such as multi-factor authentication (MFA), and applying least privilege principles.

Secure coding relies heavily on encryption to safeguard sensitive data in transit and at rest. Developers should encrypt data before being stored in databases or sent over networks using robust encryption algorithms. This guarantees that data will remain unreadable to unauthorized users even if it is intercepted or viewed without authority. Additionally, by logging pertinent information without disclosing sensitive data or system specifics, safe error handling and logging procedures assist developers in identifying and responding to possible security incidents.

Patch management and routine software updates are equally important parts of application security. Software vulnerabilities are regularly found, and to increase security measures and remedy these vulnerabilities, developers offer patches and upgrades. Patch management is the process of locating, applying, and confirming updates for all software components and applications present in the environment of an enterprise. It guarantees that systems are shielded from exploits and known flaws that attackers could use against them.

Implementing software updates on time is essential to reducing the chance of exploitation. Patches should be tested in a controlled environment before being deployed to production systems as part of an established patch management procedure within an organization. This lessens the disturbance patches create while guaranteeing they don't create new problems or interfere with already installed program configurations. Automated patch management systems can expedite this process by automatically finding and applying fixes and saving time and effort when maintaining a secure software environment.

Organizations should also give top priority to essential security fixes that fix flaws that have a significant potential impact on security. Complementary to this is vulnerability management, which evaluates and regularly scans software and systems for vulnerabilities. It assists companies in setting patching priorities according to the seriousness of vulnerabilities and the possible effects on daily operations.

In addition to fixing bugs and addressing security flaws, regular software upgrades can provide new features and performance enhancements. Organizations must weigh the necessity for security against the possible effects of upgrades on the compatibility and stability of their applications. Organizations can evaluate updates' effects before deploying them in a staging environment to guarantee business continuity.

In summary, application security is a broad field that includes efficient patch management, frequent software updates, and safe development techniques. Secure coding techniques prioritize security throughout the development lifecycle, which aids developers in creating resilient programs. Common vulnerabilities and assaults are less likely when methods like input validation, authentication, encryption, and secure error handling are used. Patch management and routine software updates are crucial for fixing recently found vulnerabilities and guaranteeing that apps are safe from changing threats. Organizations may protect sensitive data, strengthen the security posture of their applications, and uphold stakeholder and consumer trust by implementing these strategies. Maintaining a proactive approach to application security will be essential in preventing potential security breaches and vulnerabilities as cyber threats continue to advance.

CHAPTER V

Building a Robust Cyber Defense

Cyber Defense Strategies and Tactics

Organizations face an increasing threat from cyberattacks in today's linked digital ecosystem, which aims to breach their sensitive data, disrupt operations, and erode confidence. Cybersecurity experts use various techniques to prevent, identify, and address cyberattacks to reduce these risks successfully. Defense in depth and layered security are essential cybersecurity strategies enhanced by extensive incident response preparation.

A thorough cybersecurity approach known as "defense in depth" uses several tiers of protection mechanisms spread throughout an organization's IT infrastructure. Defense in depth is based on the idea of building redundant security measures so that if one layer is compromised or cannot identify an attack, further layers can offer additional protection. These layers can include application security (web application firewalls, secure coding practices), endpoint security solutions (virus software, endpoint detection and response tools), network security appliances (firewalls, intrusion detection/prevention systems), and physical security controls (surveillance, access control, and surveillance).

From preventing unwanted access to systems and data (via firewalls and access rules) to identifying and blocking malware and suspicious activity (using antivirus and behavioral analysis tools), each tier of defense in depth has a distinct function. Organizations can lower the chance of a successful breach by deploying numerous layers, which enhance the likelihood of detecting and preventing assaults at different stages of the cyber kill chain.

Layered security, sometimes confused with defense in depth, highlights the thoughtful arrangement of security controls at various IT infrastructure tiers inside an enterprise. This strategy creates overlapping layers of protection by merging different security controls and technology. In a layered security strategy, firewalls and other perimeter defenses can be combined with internal network segmentation, robust authentication methods (like multi-factor authentication), encryption of sensitive data while it's in transit, and ongoing security event monitoring and auditing.

The aim of layered security is to provide a unified and robust defense structure that tackles both internal and external threats. Network, application, endpoint, and data security measures should be diversified to help enterprises reduce vulnerabilities and exploitation risks. In addition, multilayer security complies with legal and industry best practices, guaranteeing that businesses uphold pertinent regulations (including PCI DSS, GDPR, and HIPAA) and safeguard confidential data from exposure or illegal access.

Incident response planning is another essential element of successful cyber protection tactics. Organizations need to be ready for the potential of a security breach or incident, even in the face of solid preventive efforts. Creating and recording a systematic plan for identifying, addressing, mitigating, and recovering from security incidents is known as incident response planning. Organizations can reduce the impact of accidents on their operations, reputation, and stakeholders by taking proactive planning measures.

Establishing an incident response team with clearly defined roles and responsibilities, developing incident response policies and procedures, putting incident detection and notification mechanisms (like SIEM systems and automated alerts) in place, regularly training and practicing team members, and establishing channels of communication with internal stakeholders, external partners, and regulatory authorities are all essential components of incident response planning.

Organizations depend on an incident response plan to direct their actions and efficiently coordinate their response efforts when an issue occurs. The objective is promptly returning to normal operations after containing the incident, assessing its impact and breadth, and eliminating the underlying cause. Incident response teams adhere to established workflows and escalation protocols to guarantee a prompt and well-coordinated reaction, thereby reducing downtime, data loss, and reputational harm.

In addition, incident response planning includes post-event actions like carrying out a comprehensive post-mortem analysis (also known as a lessons learned session) to find holes in the response process, revising incident response protocols in light of conclusions and suggestions, and integrating lessons learned into continuing security enhancements and training programs.

In summary, defense in depth, layered security, and incident response planning are just a few of the cyber defense strategies and methods crucial for protecting enterprises from the constantly changing cyber threat landscape. Organizations can successfully manage risks and increase their resilience to cyber-attacks by combining varied security measures and establishing numerous layers of defense systems. With incident response planning, businesses may minimize the impact on business operations and uphold stakeholder trust by being ready to detect, respond to, and recover from security incidents in a timely and coordinated manner. Adopting a proactive and strategic approach to cybersecurity is still essential in the digital era to safeguard vital assets, maintain data integrity, and ensure business continuity despite the ongoing evolution of cyber threats.

Threat Intelligence

Within cybersecurity, threat intelligence is essential for assisting enterprises in comprehending and reducing cyber-attack risks. The knowledge and understanding gleaned from examining threat data is called threat intelligence. This information helps organizations make well-informed decisions on their defensive and cybersecurity postures. By taking a proactive stance, companies can detect and address threats before they materialize into security issues.

Data collection from a variety of internal and external sources is the first step in the process of obtaining threat information. Security logs, network traffic information, endpoint telemetry, and incident reports produced by the company's IT infrastructure are examples of internal sources. These sources offer information about suspicious activity, ongoing security incidents, and possible indicators of compromise (IOCs) that point to potentially hostile activity.

A vast array of repositories and feeds that compile information from worldwide cybersecurity incidents, threat actors, malware campaigns, and vulnerabilities are included in the external threat intelligence sources category. Some sources are information sharing and analysis centers (ISACs), government agencies, commercial threat intelligence providers, open-source intelligence (OSINT) platforms, cybersecurity forums, and specialized threat intelligence communities. Organizations can obtain a broader range of threat intelligence by utilizing these external sources and improve their defenses by using the collective knowledge of the cybersecurity community.

After gathering threat data, the next stage is contextualizing and analyzing it to derive helpful intelligence. Finding patterns, trends, and correlations in the data is doing threat intelligence analysis to derive essential insights about possible risks to the company. Data mining, statistical analysis, machine learning, and human knowledge are just a few of the methods analysts employ to find new threats, comprehend threat actors' motivations and tactics, procedures, and techniques (TTPs), and evaluate the possibility and consequence of any security incidents.

The process of obtaining, evaluating, and operationalizing threat intelligence within enterprises is made much more efficient by threat intelligence platforms (TIPs). These platforms can be integrated with current cybersecurity systems and technologies to automate analysis workflows, gather threat intelligence from various sources, and promote cooperation amongst security teams. To help analysts access pertinent data and make data-driven decisions, TIPs offer centralized repositories for organizing and storing threat intelligence artifacts, including intelligence reports, threat actor profiles, and IOCs.

Data Aggregation and Enrichment. Tips gather and compile threat data from many sources, adding contextual details like threat gravity, impacted systems, and suggested countermeasures.

Automated Analysis. Tips use automation to swiftly examine massive amounts of threat data, finding patterns and connections that human analysts would miss. Automated analysis makes prioritizing alerts and concentrating human resources on high-priority risks easier.

Partnership and Exchange. By offering consolidated dashboards, incident response protocols, and platforms for exchanging threat intelligence with reliable partners and peers in the industry, TIPs help security teams work together more effectively. This kind of cooperation improves collective defense against common threats and situational awareness.

Integration with Security Tools. To automate the enforcement of security policies and response actions based on threat intelligence, TIPs integrate with SIEM platforms, endpoint detection and response (EDR) solutions, intrusion detection/prevention systems (IDS/IPS), and other security technologies.

Reporting and Visualization. To share threat intelligence findings with senior management, regulatory bodies, and stakeholders, TIPs produce individualized reports and visualizations. These reports support resource allocation, decision-making, and adherence to industry rules.

Organizations can improve their capacity to identify, address, and mitigate cyber threats by utilizing threat intelligence systems. Based on intelligence insights, these platforms allow security teams to engage in proactive threat hunting—actively looking for indications of hostile behavior within their networks. Proactively threat hunting helps organizations lower their risk of data breaches and operational interruptions by identifying and eliminating threats before they become major security incidents.

Furthermore, threat intelligence platforms facilitate the ongoing enhancement of cybersecurity defenses by offering feedback loops for enhancing security controls, upgrading incident response plans, and setting priorities for investments in mitigating emerging threats. Thanks to this iterative procedure, organizations are guaranteed to maintain their agility and resilience in the face of changing cyber threats and regulatory requirements.

In summary, threat intelligence is vital to contemporary cybersecurity operations, allowing businesses to prevent cyberattacks by employing proactive monitoring, analysis, and response. By collecting and examining threat data from many sources and using sophisticated threat intelligence systems, entities can augment their situational awareness, strengthen their ability to respond to incidents, and efficiently manage hazards. Organizations can protect their vital assets, uphold stakeholder trust, and maintain business resilience in an increasingly digital world by using threat intelligence to defend against current threats and prepare for and mitigate emerging ones.

Security Operations Centers (SOCs)

Security Operations Centers (SOCs) are vital hubs for instantly tracking, identifying, evaluating, and reacting to cybersecurity events in today's linked digital world. SOCs, or centralized operations centers, are essential for safeguarding digital assets, maintaining business continuity, and reducing cyberattacks. A SOC's primary responsibility is to protect an organization's IT infrastructure, networks, endpoints, applications, and data against cyber threats by continuously scanning these areas for indications of hostile activity.

Proactive threat detection and response is the foundation of SOC operations. To monitor and analyze security events and incidents, they make use of cutting-edge technologies like threat intelligence feeds, endpoint detection and response (EDR) solutions, intrusion prevention systems, intrusion detection and detection systems (IDS), and Security Information and Event Management (SIEM) systems. SOC analysts can quickly identify abnormalities, questionable actions, and possible security breaches through real-time correlation and analysis of large volumes of security data.

Only the first stage of SOC operations is detection. When a possible security incident is discovered, SOC analysts look into it thoroughly to determine the threat's type, extent, and significance. This study examines log files, network traffic patterns, system warnings, and other pertinent data to identify the incident's primary cause and evaluate its seriousness. SOC analysts can successfully contain and mitigate a threat by classifying incidents, prioritizing response efforts, and recommending suitable remediation activities by having a thorough grasp of threat actors' tactics, methods, and procedures (TTPs).

Reaction times represent yet another crucial facet of a SOC's operation. As soon as a security issue is verified, SOC teams move quickly to minimize damage and stop future escalation. To prevent similar situations in the future, response actions could involve putting extra security controls in place, banning malicious IP addresses, deactivating compromised accounts, installing patches or updates, and isolating vulnerable systems. Effective communication and coordination are crucial both inside the SOC and with other pertinent stakeholders, including IT teams, executive management, legal counsel, and external partners, to guarantee prompt and well-coordinated activities throughout the response phase.

A dedication to continual development, thoughtful planning, and wise investment are necessary for creating and sustaining an effective SOC. Robust cybersecurity rules and processes, roles and duties for SOC staff that are clearly defined, and extensive incident response plans that are customized to the organization's risk profile and operational requirements are fundamental components of a SOC. These plans specify the actions to be performed in the event of specific security issues, communication protocols, escalation procedures, and legal considerations.

An efficient SOC also requires a solid technological foundation. SOC technologies need to be appropriately chosen and integrated to offer thorough insight into the IT environment of the company and to enable prompt security issue identification and response. This entails implementing advanced analytics and machine learning tools to improve threat detection capabilities, integrating with threat intelligence platforms to use external threat data for proactive defense, and deploying and optimizing SIEM platforms to centralize and correlate security event data.

Continuous development is necessary to improve SOC efficacy and respond to changing cyber threats. This entails applying the knowledge gained from security incidents and industry best practices and performing routine evaluations and audits of SOC procedures, technology, and employee competencies. SOC maturity models give frameworks for assessing SOC capabilities and pinpointing areas for improvement. Examples of these models are those offered by organizations such as the National Institute of Standards and Technology (NIST) and the SANS Institute.

To sum up, Security Operations Centers (SOCs) are essential for protecting enterprises from cyberattacks because they provide proactive threat identification, quick incident response, ongoing monitoring, and efficient mitigation techniques. SOCs help firms prevent operational disruptions, safeguard sensitive data, detect and respond to security issues quickly, and uphold stakeholder trust by utilizing cutting-edge technologies, reliable procedures, and knowledgeable cybersecurity specialists. To remain ahead of developing cyber threats and maintain organizational resilience in the digital age, building and maintaining an effective SOC involves strategic planning, investment in technology and human resources, adherence to best practices, and a commitment to continuous development.

Red Team vs. Blue Team Exercises

Red Team vs. Blue Team exercises are a crucial tactic used by organizations in cybersecurity to evaluate and improve their security posture by simulating assaults and defensive tactics. These drills simulate cyberattacks and their reactions, offering priceless information about an organization's preparedness, susceptibilities, and efficacy in threat mitigation.

The idea behind Red Team vs. Blue Team exercises comes from military and intelligence settings, where Blue Teams defend against simulated attacks. At the same time, Red Teams act as enemies and try to breach fortifications. This adversarial simulation technique has been modified for use in cybersecurity to replicate real-world situations and assess an organization's capacity to identify, address, and recover from cyber threats.

Red Teams imitate malevolent actors' tactics, methods, and procedures (TTPs). They are typically made up of knowledgeable penetration testers and ethical hackers. Finding and taking advantage of weaknesses in the company's networks systems, apps, and physical security measures is their aim. Red team exercises can include phishing assaults, social engineering, exploiting system vulnerabilities, and attempts to obtain illegal access to private data or vital systems. Red Teams gives firms a comprehensive picture of their security flaws and vulnerabilities by mimicking actual attackers.

On the other hand, Blue Teams are in charge of stopping Red Team attacks and lessening the effects of fictitious catastrophes. Blue Teams comprises IT staff, cybersecurity defenders, and incident responders who monitor the organization's infrastructure, spot unusual activity, and react quickly to security events. In Red Team vs. Blue Team drills, Blue Teams use defensive technologies like network monitoring tools, endpoint detection and response (EDR) solutions, intrusion detection systems (IDS), and security information and event management (SIEM) platforms to identify and neutralize Red Team activity quickly.

Red Team versus. Blue Team exercises are crucial because they might reveal flaws and vulnerabilities that conventional security assessments might miss. A vital part of Red Team exercises is penetration testing, which goes beyond vulnerability assessment by actively using vulnerabilities to show their possible impact. Thanks to this hands-on approach, organizations receive practical insights into where their defenses are most robust and where they need to be strengthened. Organizations can lower their risk exposure and mitigate risks by proactively implementing security controls and finding vulnerabilities before bad actors exploit them.

Exercises involving Red and Blue Teams also promote cooperation and knowledge exchange among organizations. Blue Teams have practical experience tackling real-world cyberattacks, improving their incident response skills, and streamlining their security incident protocols. Through these simulated scenarios, Blue Teams can evaluate in a safe setting their incident response plans, communication procedures, and collaboration with other stakeholders, including legal counsel and executive management.

Similarly, Red Teams obtain knowledge about defensive tactics and the efficacy of security systems put in place by Blue Teams from these drills. Red Teams can strengthen their defensive capabilities against sophisticated attackers by aiding organizations by adapting their tactics and approaches to elude detection and researching how defenders identify and respond to their simulated attacks.

Lessons from Red Team vs. Blue Team exercises cover organizational preparedness, resilience, and technical skills. The exercises above underscore the significance of ongoing enhancements in cybersecurity protocols, encompassing patch management, security awareness instruction, and the deployment of defense-in-depth tactics. They also emphasize the importance of actively hunting down and monitoring dangers to identify and neutralize them before they become severe crises.

Red Team vs. Blue Team drills also support industry standards adherence and regulatory compliance. Organizations are required by several regulatory frameworks, including the General Data Protection Regulation (GDPR) and the Payment Card Industry Data Security Standard (PCI DSS), to evaluate their security measures and conduct penetration tests regularly. Red Team exercises can help firms demonstrate preventive actions, improve compliance, and lessen data breaches' financial and legal fallout.

To summarize, Red Team vs. Blue Team exercises are essential for improving cybersecurity resilience since they replicate authentic cyberattacks and defense maneuvers. Through these exercises, organizations can evaluate their security posture, find vulnerabilities, and safely test their incident response capabilities. Organizations can enhance their incident response readiness, fortify their defenses, and lessen the effect of cyberattacks by encouraging cooperation between Red Teams and Blue Teams. In the end, Red Team vs. Blue Team exercises provide a proactive approach to cybersecurity by assisting firms in keeping ahead of changing threats and successfully protecting their sensitive data and critical assets.

CHAPTER VI

Incident Response and Management

The Incident Response Lifecycle

Organizations utilize an organized process called the incident response lifecycle to handle and lessen the effects of cybersecurity incidents efficiently. It comprises several interrelated phases that lead security teams through locating, reacting to, and recovering from security breaches and cyber-attacks. These phases range from preparation and detection to containment, eradication, recovery, and lessons learned.

The first stage of the incident response lifecycle is preparation, during which businesses proactively set up the rules, guidelines, and tools required to react to security issues quickly and efficiently. This phase entails creating an incident response plan (IRP) that is specific to the risk profile of the company, outlining the duties and responsibilities of the incident response team, setting up channels of communication and escalation protocols, holding frequent drills and training sessions, and identifying critical assets and the risks that are connected with them. By being prepared, a company can reduce potential harm to its operations and reputation and ensure that it is ready to respond to problems quickly.

After discovering a security incident, the priority is to contain it to stop additional harm or illegal access to systems and data. To prevent the spread of the issue, containment procedures could include banning malicious IP addresses or domains, deactivating hacked user accounts, isolating impacted systems or networks, and putting in place temporary security controls. Effective containment minimizes the incident's impact on the organization's sensitive data and operations while also reducing the incident's breadth.

Following the incident's containment, attention turns to eliminating the security breach's primary cause from the company's IT infrastructure. Eradication is finding and removing malware, backdoors, unauthorized access points, and other security flaws that threat actors may have used to obtain access. Applying updates or patches to impacted systems, changing compromised login credentials, restoring data from clean backups, and running extensive system scans to ensure all incident traces are removed could all be necessary at this point.

After eliminating the danger, the organization starts the recovery process to get the affected systems, apps, and data back up and running. Data integrity, business continuity, and downtime are the three main goals of recovery initiatives. This could entail rebuilding or reconfiguring compromised systems, restoring data from backups, verifying system integrity, and thoroughly testing the restored systems to ensure they are safe and functional. Communication with all relevant parties—including staff members, clients, and government agencies—is essential to preserve openness and control expectations throughout this stage.

Conducting a post-event review or lessons-learned session is the last step in the incident response lifecycle, which aims to critically assess the organization's reaction to the incident. This retrospective analysis evaluates the efficacy of implemented controls and processes, pinpoints areas for development, and highlights the process's advantages and disadvantages of incident response. Documenting conclusions and suggestions, revising incident response protocols and practices in light of new information, carrying out extra training sessions and drills to close any gaps found, and disseminating lessons learned throughout the company to improve cybersecurity resilience are all important components of the lessons learned phase.

In summary, the incident response lifecycle offers an organized structure that enables businesses to efficiently anticipate, identify, address, recover from, and learn from security problems. Organizations may reduce the impact of cybersecurity breaches, save important assets, keep business operations running, and preserve stakeholder trust by adopting a systematic strategy. In today's dynamic threat landscape, ongoing improvement of incident response plans, frequent training and testing, and proactive steps to fortify defenses contribute to an organization's preparedness and resilience against changing cyber threats.

Developing an Incident Response Plan

An essential part of any organization's cybersecurity strategy is an Incident Response (IR) plan, which outlines the protocols to follow during a security incident. To reduce the impact of incidents on corporate operations and protect vital assets, it offers an organized method for identifying, responding to, mitigating, and recovering from them. The duties and responsibilities of those involved in incident response operations are clearly defined in a well-developed incident response (IR) plan, which usually consists of several essential components.

An incident response policy, which outlines the organization's dedication to safeguarding its assets, data, and systems against cybersecurity threats, is the first step in the incident response plan. This policy defines goals, sets the parameters for the incident response plan, and synchronizes incident response actions with both legal and business objectives.

Organization and Scheduling: The steps made to improve preparedness for possible incidents are covered in this section. It consists of:

Risk Assessment: Finding and evaluating any dangers and breaches to the company's data, apps, and IT infrastructure.

Incident Classification: Establishing standards for categorizing incidents according to their type, impact, and severity to prioritize response activities properly.

Team for Incident Response (IRT): assembling an incident response team with representatives from the necessary departments, including communications, cybersecurity, IT, and law. All team members, including incident coordinators, technical analysts, liaisons for communication, and legal counsel, have well-defined roles and responsibilities.

Detection and Analysis explains how to use threat intelligence feeds, endpoint detection and response (EDR) products, SIEM systems, and monitoring tools to find and analyze security occurrences. It provides instructions for:
Initial Response: Prompt action to be done as soon as an event is detected, such as alert triage, investigation, and escalation protocols.

Forensic Investigation: Investigating the incident's cause, extent, and consequences in-depth; keeping records of evidence for future use in court or investigations; and recording conclusions.

Containment, Eradication, and Recovery: Describes how to stop the problem from spreading, get rid of the underlying cause, and get the impacted systems and data back up and running normally. This comprises:

Containment Strategies: Preventing more unwanted access, restricting malicious activity, and isolating compromised systems.

Eradication Measures: Eliminating malware, security holes, or unapproved entry points found during the inquiry.

Recovery Procedures: Including adding extra security measures to prevent recurrence, verifying system integrity, and restoring systems from clean backups.

Notification and Communication: Describe notification procedures for customers, staff members, executives, internal stakeholders, and outside partners. It covers protocols for responding to media requests, making public announcements, and upholding openness throughout an incident.

Post-Incident Activities: Covers post-incident tasks like: - Lessons Learned: Performing a post-mortem study to assess the efficacy of the incident response procedure, pinpoint areas needing enhancement, and revise the incident response plan as necessary.

Documentation: Recording incident specifics, corrective measures implemented, and suggestions for managing incidents in the future.

Training and Awareness: Through continuous training and awareness initiatives, keeping staff members informed about incident response protocols, cybersecurity best practices, and new threats.

Unambiguous roles and duties facilitate efficient coordination and implementation of incident response measures during an occurrence.

Incident Coordinator: Organizes team member cooperation and communication, supervises the incident response procedure, and ensures the IR plan is followed.

Intellectual Property: To determine the origin and extent of the incident, gather and evaluate evidence, and suggest containment and recovery measures, conduct technical Analysis and forensic investigations.

Communications Liaison: Manages stakeholder notifications, media queries, and public comments to uphold transparency and reputation management. Manages both internal and external communication.

Legal Advisor: Offers legal advice on data protection, compliance, and the legal ramifications of incident response procedures.

IT Support: Offers system administrators, network engineers, and database administrators technical assistance for putting containment, eradication, and recovery procedures into action.

Each position is crucial to the incident response lifecycle to minimize disruption, manage risks, and safeguard the organization's assets and reputation. Maintaining preparedness and resilience against changing cyber threats requires frequent testing, simulated exercises, and revisions to the incident response plan based on lessons acquired from prior occurrences. Organizations can improve their capacity to identify, address, and recover from security incidents quickly and efficiently by investing in a thorough incident response strategy and providing skilled staff with the necessary authority to carry out their duties.

Incident Detection and Analysis

Cybersecurity operations require effective incident detection and analysis for enterprises to quickly identify security problems and take appropriate action before they become serious breaches. Monitoring IT infrastructure, networks, endpoints, and applications continuously for abnormalities, malicious activity, unauthorized access, and other indications of compromise (IOCs) is known as incident detection. This proactive approach depends on reliable real-time monitoring and alerting technologies to identify security events and launch prompt reaction measures.

By giving an organization's digital environment visibility and raising alarms for suspicious activity or departures from typical behavior, monitoring, and alerting technologies are essential to incident detection. Logs and events from a variety of sources, including firewalls, intrusion detection/prevention systems (IDS/IPS), endpoint detection and response (EDR) tools, and network traffic monitors, are frequently centralized and correlated using Security Information and Event Management (SIEM) systems. SIEM platforms use predefined rules, signatures, and behavioral analytics to identify possible security events based on patterns that point to malicious activity, like unauthorized access, unusual login attempts, malware infections, and efforts to exfiltrate data.

Security analysts perform first triage to determine the type and seriousness of warnings they get from monitoring systems. This procedure entails confirming the legitimacy of the alert, figuring out if it's a real security issue, and ranking incidents according to how they might affect the organization's operations and data integrity. Incident response teams adhere to predetermined procedures and escalation protocols to minimize the danger of further compromise and guarantee that significant occurrences are swiftly addressed.

Forensic investigation and evidence gathering are crucial elements of incident response to comprehend the underlying cause, extent, and consequences of security incidents. Forensic analysts use specific methods and equipment to collect and evaluate digital evidence, maintain a chain of custody, and create a timeline of events leading up to and during the incident. System logs, memory dumps, network traffic captures, file system information, and other artifacts are examined as part of digital forensics to determine how the incident happened, what data was accessed or compromised, and the threat actors' tactics, methods, and procedures (TTPs).

Preserving the integrity and confidentiality of evidence is essential during forensic analysis to facilitate future legal or regulatory inquiries. This entails abiding by the best standards for handling evidence, including keeping track of audit trails, recording gathering techniques, and ensuring that gathered data is acceptable in court when needed. Forensic analysts work closely with incident response teams, attorneys, and law enforcement organizations when protecting evidence and assisting with incident cleanup.

Moreover, digital forensics plays a critical role in incident recovery by offering insights into compromised, exploited systems and possible repair paths. The analysis results can guide decisions on incident response, including updating or patching susceptible systems, tightening access restrictions, and putting extra security measures in place to stop recurrence. Organizations can reduce future risks caused by similar threats, strengthen incident response capabilities, and improve overall cybersecurity posture by utilizing forensic analysis.

To sum up, incident detection and analysis are essential components of efficient cybersecurity operations that help companies identify, address, and minimize security problems promptly and efficiently. Robust monitoring and alerting systems backed by cutting-edge technology like behavioral analytics and SIEM systems provide visibility into the company's digital environment and make it easier to identify suspicious activity early on. To guide incident response activities and support remediation plans, forensic analysis and evidence collecting offer crucial insights into the nature and impact of security occurrences. Organizations can enhance their resilience against evolving cyber threats, safeguard sensitive data, and uphold stakeholder trust in an increasingly interconnected and threat-prone digital landscape by allocating resources toward proactive monitoring, alerting mechanisms, and digital forensics capabilities.

Post-Incident Activities

Following the effective containment and mitigation of a cybersecurity incident, an organization must undertake several crucial post-event measures to guarantee a thorough recovery, promote organizational learning, and bolster resilience against similar occurrences. The tasks above comprise processes related to reporting and documentation, attempts towards recovery, and a comprehensive post-event evaluation aimed at extracting lessons learned and enhancing incident response capabilities.

Thoroughly reporting and documenting the incident details, reaction actions, and results is essential to post-incident activity.

Depending on the circumstances and relevant laws, organizations could be required to notify industry authorities, data protection agencies, or regulatory bodies about security issues. Efficient and precise documentation guarantees adherence to legal duties and prevents possible legal or monetary sanctions.

Executive management, stakeholders, and pertinent departments must be informed about the incident's impact, remediation efforts, and lessons gained internally through thorough incident reports and documentation.

Accountability, awareness of cybersecurity risks, and a proactive approach to strengthening organizational defenses are all facilitated by clear and honest communication.

Incident reporting and recordkeeping facilitate Building a centralized knowledge base of past incidents, reaction plans, and practical mitigation approaches. Organizations can use this knowledge base to improve incident response procedures, hone incident response plans, and strengthen overall cybersecurity posture by utilizing past experiences and best practices.

The organization's attention is diverted to recovery operations once a security incident has been contained and mitigated to get the impacted systems, apps, and data back up and running normally.

System restoration involves rebuilding or restoring compromised systems from clean backups, with extra care taken to ensure that any malware or unauthorized access points found during the incident are removed from the restored systems.

Checking that the recovered data is complete and undamaged, ensuring that no critical information was lost or tampered with during the occurrence.

Return impacted services and apps to production environments gradually while looking for any lingering problems or performance deterioration.

Keeping staff, clients, and business partners informed on the status of recovery efforts, anticipated timeframes for service restoration, and any necessary safety measures or actions regularly.

IT teams, cybersecurity experts, and other pertinent stakeholders must work together to reduce downtime, restore business continuity, and lessen the incident's financial and operational effects to recover effectively.

Organizations can hasten the restoration to regular operations and minimize business disruptions by assuring thorough validation of restored systems and data and prioritizing recovery actions based on criticality.

Review Following Incident: Conducting a comprehensive post-mortem or post-incident review is the last step in the post-event process. Its purpose is to evaluate how the organization handled the incident, pinpoint areas of strength and weakness in the incident response procedures, and draw lessons learned for better incident management in the future.

Root Cause Analysis: Examining the underlying causes and contributing elements, such as system flaws or gaps in the security mechanisms already in place, that resulted in the incident.

Effectiveness Assessment: Analyzing incident response protocols, such as detection, containment, eradication, and recovery actions, to see where improvements can be made.

Acquired Knowledge: Updating incident response plans, changing security policies, and strengthening cybersecurity defenses require recording insights, observations, and suggestions from incident response experience.

Training and Awareness: Putting in place focused training courses and awareness campaigns for incident response teams and other pertinent staff members to close skills gaps found, enhance incident management abilities and promote a culture of cybersecurity vigilance and awareness.

Organizations can turn incident response experiences into chances for ongoing development and resilience-building by conducting a thorough post-event review. Future incident response plans that incorporate the knowledge gained from previous events improve readiness, fortify incident response skills, and lessen the probability and effect of cybersecurity issues in the future.

In conclusion, efficient post-event procedures are critical for businesses to recover from cybersecurity breaches quickly, thoroughly record incident information, and extract insightful knowledge that improves incident response skills. Organizations can reduce the impact of events on business operations, adhere to regulatory requirements, and promote a proactive approach to cybersecurity resilience by implementing rigorous recovery efforts, systematic post-incident evaluations, and precise reporting and documentation. In an increasingly digital and linked world, firms can adapt to changing cyber threats, safeguard vital assets, and uphold stakeholder trust by continuously improving incident response procedures based on lessons gained.

CHAPTER VII

Cybersecurity Compliance and Legal Issues

Overview of Cybersecurity Regulations

In a world going digital, cybersecurity laws are becoming more and more critical since protecting sensitive data is crucial. These laws are intended to protect information, guarantee privacy, and uphold the integrity of systems in several different sectors. Strict data protection and privacy guidelines are established by essential laws like the Health Insurance Portability and Accountability Act (HIPAA) and the General Data Protection Regulation (GDPR). A complete approach to cybersecurity is ensured by the various industries' specific compliance requirements, customized to their particular risks and requirements.

One of the world's most extensive and comprehensive data protection laws was enacted by the European Union in 2018 and is known as the General Data Protection Regulation (GDPR). By uniting data protection rules across the EU, it seeks to offer individuals control over their data and streamline the regulatory environment for global business. Regardless of the organization's location, GDPR applies to any processing of personal data about EU individuals. Important clauses include the need to obtain an individual's express consent before collecting their data, the right of individuals to access their data, the right to have their data erased or forgotten, and the necessity that enterprises notify data breaches to individuals within 72 hours. Heavy penalties for noncompliance may reach 20 million euros or 4% of the yearly global turnover, whichever is higher. The California Consumer Privacy Act

(CCPA) in the United States and other data protection legislation worldwide have been influenced by GDPR, which has established a global standard.

Enacted in 1996, the Health Insurance Portability and Accountability Act (HIPAA) strongly emphasizes safeguarding private patient data. The HIPAA Privacy Rule establishes guidelines for the security of health information, guaranteeing that patient data is appropriately protected while permitting the exchange of health information required to deliver high-quality medical care. Organizations must use technological and non-technical measures to protect individuals' electronic protected health information (ePHI), as the Security Rule specifies. Healthcare clearinghouses, health plans, providers, and business partners handling sensitive health data must comply with HIPAA. Significant consequences, such as fines and, in extreme circumstances, criminal prosecutions, might result from violations.

Different industries have unique compliance requirements based on their risks and these general standards. For instance, the United States Gramm-Leach-Bliley Act (GLBA), which requires financial firms to disclose their information-sharing policies and protect sensitive data, applies to the banking sector. Another essential rule in this field is the Payment Card Industry Data Security Standard (PCI DSS), which establishes operational and technical specifications for businesses that accept or process payments to safeguard cardholder data.

The federal government also imposes cybersecurity restrictions on its contractors through guidelines like the Federal Information Security Management Act (FISMA) and the National Institute of Standards and Technology (NIST) Special Publication 800-171. NIST 800-171 recommends safeguarding controlled unclassified information (CUI) in non-federal systems and organizations. At the same time, FISMA mandates that federal agencies create, record, and carry out an information security and protection policy. To protect the security of federal information, contractors and subcontractors doing business with federal agencies must abide by these guidelines.

The Federal Communications Commission (FCC) enforces rules in the telecommunications sector to safeguard secure communications networks and consumer privacy. Telecommunications providers are required by the Communications Assistance for Law Enforcement Act (CALEA) to support law enforcement in carrying out electronic surveillance while upholding communications security and privacy.

On a global scale, several nations have created their cybersecurity laws. For example, China's Cybersecurity Law (CSL), which went into effect in 2017, requires network products and services used in critical information infrastructure to undergo security evaluations and to adhere to stringent data localization rules. Similarly, corporations must notify individuals and the Australian Information Commissioner about data breaches likely to cause substantial harm under Australia's Notifiable Data Breaches (NDB) scheme, a component of the Privacy Act 1988.

To sum up, cybersecurity laws are essential for safeguarding private data and maintaining security in various sectors. Stricter standards are created by critical regulations like GDPR and HIPAA, which impact worldwide practices and propel the creation of industry-specific compliance requirements. These rules improve security and confidence in the digital ecosystem while protecting people and businesses. The regulatory environment will change along with cyber risks, so companies must remain alert and flexible in their compliance activities.

Legal Implications of Cyber Incidents

Organizations in every industry are impacted by cyber events' intricate and constantly changing legal ramifications. An effective cybersecurity strategy must consider addressing data breaches, complying with reporting requirements, and comprehending liabilities and legal threats. Organizations must negotiate a problematic legal environment as cyber threats increase in sophistication and regularity to shield themselves from severe financial, reputational, and legal repercussions.

In the context of cyber incidents, liability is a complex matter. Determining who is legally liable for a data breach or hack can be difficult. Several parties may be held accountable, such as the company that experienced the breach, outside service providers, and even some company employees. The main legal risks include contractual penalties, regulatory fines, and possible lawsuits from impacted parties or persons. It is expected of organizations to protect data with appropriate security procedures. Negligence claims may be made if this is not done. For example, a firm might be held accountable for damages arising from a breach if it disregards industry standards for data protection. Furthermore, if a company gives a false image of its cybersecurity posture, it may be accused of engaging in dishonest business activities, which could result in additional legal action.

Effectively managing data breaches is essential to reducing legal risks. Organizations that experience a breach must respond quickly to determine the extent of the harm, stop the violation, and prevent additional unauthorized access. An extensive investigation is usually required to ascertain the breach type, the data accessed, and the attackers' strategies. To guarantee that the reaction is both technically sound and compliant with the law, it is imperative to involve cybersecurity specialists and legal counsel early in the process. A business may prove it took the right actions to handle the issue by having a well-documented response plan, which can help it in future legal procedures.

One of the most essential parts of managing data breaches is reporting requirements. Several laws and regulations require organizations to notify the public, regulatory agencies and impacted parties of violations. The requirements differ based on the industry and jurisdiction. For instance, enterprises must notify the appropriate supervisory body of specific data breaches within 72 hours of becoming aware of them under the General Data Protection Regulation (GDPR) in the European Union. If there is a significant risk that the breach would violate someone's rights or liberties, they must also inform the impacted parties. The US Health Insurance Portability and Accountability Act (HIPAA) mandates that covered companies report breaches involving unprotected protected health information to the Department of Health and Human Services and the impacted individuals.

Organizations must also consider the consequences of cyber incidents for contracts. These days, breach notification clauses and particular cybersecurity standards are found in many contracts. Violating these contractual duties may give rise to claims of breach of contract and related damages. Organizations must ensure that their cybersecurity procedures comply with contractual obligations by carefully reviewing their contracts. This includes being aware of indemnity provisions that can mandate that one party pay the other's losses from a cyber event.

Organizations need to be mindful of the possibility of civil action stemming from cyber incidents and regulatory and contractual obligations. Affected parties may bring class-action lawsuits to recover damages for losses resulting from a data breach. Potential settlements or judgments in these cases could reach substantial sums of money, making them time-consuming and expensive. To successfully defend against such claims, it can be essential to show that the company implemented reasonable measures to secure data and appropriately handled the breach.

To sum up, there are many other legal ramifications associated with cyber incidents, such as reporting requirements, responsibility, and how to handle data breaches. Organizations need to negotiate a complicated legal environment to safeguard themselves from severe financial, reputational, and legal repercussions. Organizations may lessen the effects of cyber events and protect their operations in an increasingly digital world by being aware of their legal risks, putting strong cybersecurity measures in place, and ensuring reporting regulations are followed.

Cyber Insurance

Cyber insurance has emerged as a crucial instrument for businesses aiming to reduce the financial risks connected to cyber events. Comprehensive protection against potential losses is more important than ever as cyber threats become more sophisticated. Cyber insurance is a safety net, providing monetary damages for various cyber-related losses. It is imperative to comprehend the advantages and constraints of cyber insurance and to assess, choose, and implement suitable coverage that caters to the company's particular requirements.

Financial protection against a range of cyber dangers is one of the main advantages of cyber insurance. Policies usually cover costs related to data breaches, including legal fees, credit monitoring services for impacted individuals, notification costs, and PR efforts to minimize reputational harm. Cyber insurance can also pay for the expenses of a cyberattack-related company interruption, making up for any lost revenue. This coverage feature benefits companies that depend significantly on digital activities, where even a brief disruption can have significant financial ramifications. Moreover, a lot of policies include coverage for ransomware attacks, which includes charges for both paying the ransom and restoring systems and data.

Cyber insurance covers common cyber threats

Access to knowledge and tools that can support an organization's response to and recovery from a cyber event is another critical benefit of cyber insurance. Legal advice, forensic investigators, and incident response teams are some of the support services that insurers frequently provide. In the early wake of an assault, these tools can be beneficial in containing the breach, evaluating the damage, and fulfilling reporting obligations to the relevant authorities. Insurers may also offer risk management services, such as cybersecurity evaluations and training courses, to help businesses fortify their defenses and lower the probability of upcoming mishaps.

After completing the risk assessment, firms can start comparing various cyber insurance plans. Comparing policies from several insurers is crucial, considering elements like rates, exclusions, policy limits, and coverage scope. Policies that give the flexibility to modify coverage as needs change and comprehensive coverage for their most significant risks should be sought after by organizations. It can be helpful to speak with a broker specializing in cyber insurance since they can offer professional advice and assist in navigating the intricacies of the insurance industry.

Organizations should assess the insurer's standing and financial soundness in addition to the coverage offered by various policies. A reputable insurer with a solid track record of managing cyber claims can provide more comfort that the claims procedure will be quick and equitable. To make sure that the insurer's claims procedure and support offerings meet the requirements and expectations of the company, it is also crucial to evaluate them.

Choosing the right cyber insurance is a continuous rather than a one-time choice. It is crucial to routinely examine and update the insurance policy to ensure it stays in line with current risks as cyber threats change and the organization's risk profile shifts. This could entail changing the maximum amount of coverage, adding endorsements for particular risks, or even changing insurers if better alternatives emerge.

To sum up, cyber insurance provides several advantages, such as access to professional resources and financial security, that can assist businesses in mitigating the risks involved in cyber disasters. However, it has certain restrictions that need to be carefully considered, such as possible coverage gaps and exclusions. A complete grasp of the organization's risk profile, a thorough comparison of various policies, and continual assessment and adjustment to guarantee continuous alignment with the organization's needs are necessary for evaluating and choosing the proper coverage. Organizations can strengthen their resistance to cyberattacks and better safeguard their operations in a world that is becoming increasingly digital by adopting a strategic approach to cyber insurance.

Ethical Considerations in Cybersecurity

In a world where digital interactions rule both personal and professional lives, ethical questions in cybersecurity are becoming more and more significant. The fundamental ideas behind these issues are the harmony between security and privacy, the function of ethical hacking, and responsible disclosure. Cybersecurity experts must negotiate challenging ethical terrain to ensure that their actions support both security and individual rights as they work to safeguard confidential data and preserve the integrity of digital systems.

One of the central ethical problems in cybersecurity is balancing privacy with security. On the one hand, strong security measures are necessary to shield data against intrusions, hacks, and other nefarious activity. However, these actions frequently call for access to private data, which may violate someone's right to privacy. Implementing thorough monitoring systems, for example, might aid in identifying and preventing unwanted access, but it may also entail closely examining user behavior, raising questions about data usage and surveillance. Finding the ideal balance necessitates a sophisticated strategy that considers the context and goal of security measures, making sure they are appropriate and, to the maximum extent feasible, respecting people's privacy.

Another essential component of cybersecurity ethics is ethical hacking, sometimes called penetration testing or white-hat hacking. Before malevolent hackers take advantage of system vulnerabilities, ethical hackers utilize their expertise to find and fix them. In addition to raising ethical concerns regarding consent and the possibility of unintentional injury, this proactive strategy is essential for improving security. Before testing, ethical hackers must acquire express permission from the owners of the systems and operate within legal boundaries. With this consent, all parties concerned may be sure that their activities are allowed and that they know the potential dangers and advantages.

In addition, ethical hacking calls for a dedication to responsible disclosure. The moral problem that arises when ethical hackers locate vulnerabilities is how to reveal their findings. To practice responsible disclosure, a vendor or impacted organization must be notified privately of the vulnerability and allowed to address it before any information is made public. In contrast, full disclosure involves making the vulnerability known to the public immediately, possibly endangering systems before a fix is even available. Responsible disclosure encourages a cooperative effort to improve cybersecurity by balancing the public's right to know about security flaws and the necessity of shielding systems from instant attacks.

The ethical hacking and responsible disclosure tenets emphasize the broader ethical requirement for responsibility and transparency in cybersecurity. Professionals in cybersecurity must conduct themselves honorably, putting the public interest ahead of their interests or notoriety. This dedication is especially crucial when cyber threats pose societal and political problems and technological difficulties. For instance, there may be significant repercussions for democracy, freedom, and human rights if governments or corporations misuse personal data. Therefore, cybersecurity experts must promote moral principles that uphold people's rights and foster confidence in digital systems.

The ethical issues in cybersecurity go beyond ethical hacking to include creating and applying new technology. For example, machine learning and artificial intelligence

(AI) are being utilized increasingly to improve security by anticipating risks and identifying anomalies. But these technologies also raise moral concerns about responsibility, justice, and bias. Artificial intelligence (AI) systems may unintentionally reinforce preexisting biases in data, producing biased results. Professionals in the field of cybersecurity need to make sure that their systems and tools are developed and applied in a fair, transparent, and responsible manner. They must also audit and update them frequently to keep them free from bias and guarantee they fulfill their intended purposes without violating anyone's rights.

Furthermore, ethical issues in cybersecurity extend beyond technical procedures to include broader company cultures. Companies must encourage people to prioritize the ethical problems in their work by fostering an environment that values ethics and responsibility. Establishing explicit norms and procedures for moral behavior, offering training on moral matters, and encouraging an atmosphere in which ethical questions can be asked and answered without fear of reprisal are all part of this culture. Cybersecurity leaders must exemplify moral conduct by committing to honesty, openness, and the common good.

Legal and regulatory compliance is another area where cybersecurity and ethics collide. Although laws and regulations offer a structure for moral behavior, they frequently need to catch up to the rapid evolution of technology. In addition to abiding by the law, cybersecurity experts should push for revisions and enhancements to legal frameworks that more effectively handle modern issues. As part of this advocacy, one may participate in policy talks, help create standards and guidelines, and collaborate with regulators to ensure cybersecurity procedures uphold people's rights and advance society's welfare.

To sum up, ethical issues in cybersecurity include the careful balancing act between privacy and security, ethical hacking standards and responsible disclosure, and the broader ramifications of organizational culture and technology breakthroughs. Cybersecurity professionals must handle these challenging ethical situations with honesty, openness, and dedication to the general welfare. The cybersecurity sector may improve security while upholding individual rights and encouraging confidence in digital systems by emphasizing ethical norms and promoting a culture of accountability. This all-encompassing strategy is necessary to solve the complex cybersecurity threats in a world growing more interconnected daily.

CHAPTER VIII

Cybersecurity in the Age of Cloud Computing

The Shift to Cloud Computing

Businesses now work in a completely new way thanks to the cloud, which offers many advantages but presents several difficulties. Cloud computing enables enterprises to use cutting-edge services and technology that improve productivity, scalability, and creativity. To guarantee a seamless and safe deployment, the move to cloud environments also necessitates careful evaluation of numerous risks and challenges.

The cost-effectiveness of cloud computing is one of its main advantages. Significant capital expenditures on hardware, software, and maintenance are frequently associated with traditional IT infrastructure. On the other hand, pay-as-you-go cloud services let businesses pay only for the resources they use. Budgeting becomes more predictable, and upfront costs are decreased with this operational expenditure model. Furthermore, cloud providers manage upgrades and maintenance, freeing your internal IT staff to concentrate on more critical tasks.

Another significant benefit of cloud computing is scalability. Cloud services do not require significant hardware investments, allowing organizations to adapt to growth or consumption changes. They may be swiftly scaled up or down to suit changing demands. This scalability is very helpful for startups and small to medium-sized businesses (SMEs) that could see seasonal fluctuations in their workloads or quick expansion. These businesses may effectively manage their IT requirements and minimize the risk of over- or under-provisioning by utilizing cloud resources.

Cloud computing also improves teamwork and accessibility. Cloud services facilitate remote work and collaboration among geographically distributed teams by granting employees access to data and apps from any location with an internet connection. Since workers can now more readily share information and work together in real time, this enhanced accessibility may result in higher productivity and creativity. Cloud providers provide collaboration solutions like document sharing and project management software to improve team chemistry and productivity further.

Another significant advantage of adopting the cloud is innovation. Modern technologies like artificial intelligence (AI), machine learning, and big data analytics are accessible through cloud platforms and can lead to competitive advantage and company transformation. These sophisticated tools enable businesses to create new goods and services, automate procedures, and analyze vast amounts of data. Innovation and agility are promoted when new technologies may be swiftly tested and implemented without requiring a large initial outlay.

Even with these advantages, moving to cloud computing has several drawbacks. One of the main issues is privacy and data security. There are hazards associated with data breaches and illegal access while storing confidential data on the cloud. Organizations must guarantee that their cloud providers incorporate robust security protocols, like encryption, multi-factor authentication, and periodic security audits. Furthermore, companies must abide by applicable data protection laws, such as the General Data Protection Regulation (GDPR) in Europe, which sets tight guidelines for processing and storing data.

The complexity of migration is another obstacle to cloud adoption. Moving from on-premises infrastructure to the cloud necessitates meticulous planning and implementation to minimize disruptions and guarantee data integrity. Re-architecting workflows and apps to be compatible with cloud settings is a common step in this approach that can be resource- and time-intensive. The possibility of vendor lock-in, in which reliance on the services and technologies of a single cloud provider makes it challenging to transfer providers or return to on-premises solutions, must also be taken into account by organizations.

Managing costs is yet another possible difficulty. Although cloud computing might be economical, it must be carefully managed and monitored to prevent unforeseen costs. The pay-as-you-go model may result in cost overruns if resources are not adequately handled. This is especially true when unexpected demand spikes or decommissioned resources are not. Organizations must implement robust cost management procedures to ensure they stay under budget. These procedures include limiting consumption, checking invoices often, and using cloud cost optimization technologies.

The adoption of cloud computing also requires careful consideration of governance and compliance. Businesses must ensure that their cloud operations adhere to industry-specific rules and guidelines, which might differ significantly between sectors. This compliance encompasses concerns about data residency, cross-border data transfers, and privacy and data protection. Effective governance structures are essential to handle these intricacies and guarantee that cloud operations comply with corporate guidelines and legal obligations.

Additionally, a change in corporate culture and skill sets is necessary to transition to cloud computing. IT workers must acquire new skills and expertise to operate cloud systems, which might differ significantly from traditional on-premises infrastructure. Acquiring new competencies may necessitate funding for employee upskilling through training and development programs. The principles of cloud computing, such as agility, adaptability, and continual improvement, must also be embraced by company culture.

To sum up, there are a lot of advantages to moving to cloud computing, such as increased accessibility, scalability, cost-effectiveness, and access to cutting-edge technologies. However, it also brings difficulties with data security, complex migrations, cost control, compliance, and the requirement for new skills and cultural shifts. Employers must carefully consider these advantages and disadvantages before implementing a cloud strategy to optimize cloud adoption benefits and minimize associated risks. By doing this, businesses can effectively manage the shift to cloud computing and use its advantages to spur innovation and corporate expansion.

Cloud Security Best Practices

As more and more businesses depend on cloud computing for vital operations, cloud security best practices are crucial for protecting cloud infrastructure and services. A multifaceted strategy is needed to secure the cloud, addressing many components of the cloud environment, such as data protection, identity and access management (IAM), threat detection, and regulatory compliance. Strong security measures must be implemented to safeguard private data, guarantee service availability, and uphold client confidence.

Securing the cloud infrastructure is a core component of cloud security. The first step is choosing a trustworthy cloud service provider (CSP) that satisfies legal requirements and industry standards while providing robust security measures. Potential CSPs should have security certifications from organizations like ISO 27001,

SOC 2, and PCI DSS to ensure they follow best risk management practices and data protection practices. Organizations need to set up their cloud environment safely after choosing a CSP. This entails using safe essential management procedures, establishing virtual private networks (VPNs), and implementing robust encryption techniques for data in transit and at rest.

Effective identity and access management (IAM) is essential in the cloud environment and safeguarding the cloud infrastructure. Ensuring that only authorized users have access to sensitive data and systems is the goal of identity and access management (IAM). The minor privilege concept states that users should only be given the minimal access required to carry out their job duties, which is the first step in putting effective IAM practices into practice. As a result, there is a lower chance of unwanted access and less chance of compromised accounts causing harm.

IAM's multi-factor authentication (MFA) is a crucial element that raises the security ante. To obtain access, users of MFA must supply two or more verification elements, such as a password, a security token, or biometric verification. MFA dramatically improves security and lowers the possibility of successful phishing attempts and credential theft by demanding multiple forms of authentication.

RBAC, or role-based access control, is yet another crucial IAM tactic. RBAC ensures that access rights align with job responsibilities by allocating permissions according to user roles within the company. The danger of privilege escalation is decreased and access control is made simpler using this method. To take into account changes in roles and responsibilities and to revoke access for former workers or contractors, businesses should also routinely evaluate and update their access restrictions.

Monitoring and auditing are crucial IAM procedures to identify and address unwanted access attempts and other questionable activity. Continuous monitoring systems that give real-time insight into user behavior and access patterns should be used by organizations. When these systems detect unusual activity, such as repeated failed login attempts or access from strange places, they can produce alerts, which lets security teams look into it and take appropriate action quickly. Frequent audits of permissions and access logs assist in detecting possible vulnerabilities and ensuring adherence to security guidelines.

Another crucial component of cloud security is data protection. Robust encryption techniques must be used by organizations to safeguard data while it is in transit and at rest. Data encryption ensures that information is unreadable and unusable even if it is intercepted or viewed without authority. Data loss prevention (DLP) solutions, in addition to encryption, can aid in tracking and managing sensitive data transit inside the cloud environment, preventing unauthorized sharing or transfer.

Because endpoints like laptops, cellphones, and IoT devices frequently act as entry points for cyber threats, endpoint security is equally essential in the cloud. Endpoint protection solutions, including intrusion detection systems, firewalls, and antivirus software, can be implemented to protect these devices and stop them from being used as attack vectors against the cloud infrastructure. Software and firmware must be patched and updated regularly to fix known vulnerabilities and lower the chance of exploitation.

An all-encompassing cloud security plan must include threat detection and response. Advanced threat detection tools, including intrusion detection systems (IDS), security information and event management (SIEM) programs, and anomaly detection based on artificial intelligence (AI), should be implemented by organizations. Before possible dangers may do a great deal of harm, these techniques assist in identifying and reducing their impact. To guarantee that the company can respond to security issues efficiently, reduce their impact, and recover swiftly, incident response strategies ought to be created and routinely verified.

Another critical cloud security component is adherence to industry best practices and regulatory regulations. Businesses need to be aware of the rules specific to their sector and ensure that their cloud environment complies with these requirements. This entails carrying out frequent risk assessments, keeping thorough records of security controls and guidelines, and allowing independent third parties to audit your company regularly. In addition to protecting sensitive data, compliance increases stakeholder and customer trust.

To sum up, cloud security best practices are critical for safeguarding cloud services and infrastructure against various cyberattacks. Securing the cloud infrastructure, putting in place strong identity and access control procedures, protecting data with encryption and DLP, ensuring endpoints are secure, and putting advanced threat detection and response tools to use are all examples of adequate security measures. Frequent surveillance, examinations, and adherence to legal requirements all contribute to improving the cloud environment's security posture. Organizations may protect sensitive data, reduce risks, and ensure the availability and integrity of their cloud services by implementing these best practices.

Hybrid and Multi-Cloud Environments

Managing security across several cloud providers has become more complex with the introduction of hybrid and multi-cloud setups. As more and more businesses use the distinct benefits offered by various cloud services, maintaining a stable and reliable security posture becomes critical. To properly handle security concerns, hybrid cloud environments—which integrate private and public clouds—and multi-cloud strategies—which use services from many cloud providers—require careful design, cutting-edge tools, and all-encompassing tactics.

Understanding each cloud provider's distinct security models and obligations is the first step toward managing security across different providers. Cloud service providers use a shared responsibility model in which the client protects their data and apps in the cloud. In contrast, the provider oversees the security of the cloud infrastructure. Because each provider has a different responsibility split, it's essential to comprehend each provider's security policies and controls. Companies must perform extensive due diligence, assessing each service's security credentials, compliance with applicable laws, and other factors.

Incident response and monitoring capabilities need to be modified for hybrid and multi-cloud environments. Employing sophisticated monitoring solutions that offer thorough insight into all cloud services will help organizations identify unusual activity and any security risks. To ensure that the company can react to security issues promptly and efficiently, incident response plans should be revised to consider the complexities of hybrid and multi-cloud environments. To reduce the effect of security breaches, coordination between response teams located on-premises and in the cloud is essential.

In summary, handling security in hybrid and multi-cloud settings necessitates a comprehensive strategy that considers these configurations' particular difficulties. An effective security strategy must include endpoint security measures, flexible network security, strong IAM regulations, centralized security management frameworks, and comprehensive data protection procedures. Compliance management, sophisticated monitoring, and incident response capabilities further improve the organization's capacity to safeguard its cloud infrastructure and services. By implementing these recommended practices and utilizing suitable tools, enterprises can attain a hybrid and multi-cloud environment that is both secure and robust, thereby optimizing cloud computing advantages while reducing related risks.

Case Studies: Cloud Security Incidents

There are several advantages to the growing reliance on cloud computing, including improved scalability, cost savings, and flexibility. It has, nevertheless, also brought forward fresh security issues. Enterprises must get insights from real-world cloud security incidents to comprehend potential dangers and implement effective solutions to protect their cloud systems. Analyzing prominent cloud security incidents offers insightful information about what leads to breaches and how companies can improve their security posture.

Capital One experienced one of the cloud security breaches that received the most significant media attention in 2019. A former employee of Amazon Web Services (AWS) exploited a misconfigured web application firewall (WAF) to get unauthorized access to Capital One's data hosted on AWS. Over 100 million customers' names, addresses, credit scores, and social security numbers were revealed due to the hack. This event brought to light how crucial it is to secure cloud setups. Serious data breaches can result from configuration errors, such as leaving default settings unmodified or putting access controls incorrectly. Organizations must continually audit and monitor their cloud installations to guarantee adherence to best security practices and reduce the possibility of human mistakes.

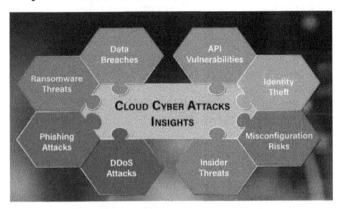

Another noteworthy event in 2017 concerned Verizon and the release of customer data due to a misconfigured AWS S3 storage bucket. An employee made the error of setting the access permissions to "public," which allowed anyone with the URL to view the data, which led to the breach. This event emphasizes the importance of stringent access control procedures and adequate training for staff members who handle cloud resources. Essential measures to avoid unwanted access include ensuring sensitive data is kept in private buckets with the proper access rights and routinely checking these settings.

Another event with significant lessons is the 2017 Dow Jones data leak. The personal information of millions of users was accidentally made public by a third-party contractor who set up an AWS S3 bucket for public access. This incident serves as a reminder of the dangers posed by using unreliable third parties and the necessity of strict vendor control procedures. Companies need to make sure outside vendors follow security guidelines, screen them carefully, and keep an eye on who has access to critical information. The dangers of data breaches can be reduced by putting in place robust contractual agreements with precise security criteria and by regularly evaluating third-party vendors' security.

A hack involving the marketing company Exactis in 2018 exposed about 340 million records, including private data like phone numbers, email addresses, and physical addresses. An unsecured Elasticsearch database housed in the cloud was the source of the breach. This event highlights how important it is to secure cloud-based databases and other storage systems. Organizations should encrypt information while it's in transit and at rest to prevent unwanted access to sensitive data. Securing cloud-based storage also requires implementing robust authentication methods and restricting database access using the least privilege concept.

Uber's 2016 data hack, which wasn't made public until 2017, is a crucial lesson in the value of openness and prompt breach notice. Hackers gained access to an Uber software engineer's private GitHub repository and took credentials to access data hosted on AWS. Fifty-seven million users' and drivers' personal information was compromised. Uber faced severe reputational harm and legal ramifications for its choice to hide the breach and pay the hackers to remove the data rather than alerting the impacted parties and authorities. This story emphasizes how important it is for businesses to follow breach notification regulations and have well-defined incident response plans. Timely disclosure and transparent communication can lessen the impact of a breach and maintain trust with customers and stakeholders.

Organizations should take a holistic approach incorporating technical, administrative, and physical controls to deploy successful cloud security measures and learn from these instances. To begin with, frequent security audits and assessments are necessary to find and fix vulnerabilities in cloud installations. Security policy compliance can be guaranteed, and misconfigurations can be seen with automated technologies. Continuous monitoring systems can also offer real-time visibility into cloud settings, facilitating the prompt detection and handling of security incidents.

Second, access management is one of the most important aspects of cloud security. Organizations should use robust authentication measures like multi-factor authentication (MFA) to safeguard access to cloud resources. To ensure that users have the minimal amount of rights required to carry out their responsibilities, role-based access control, or RBAC, should be implemented. Reviewing access rights regularly can help avoid privilege creep and lower the danger of insider threats.

Thirdly, the security of sensitive data in the cloud depends on data protection techniques like tokenization and encryption. Businesses must ensure that encryption keys are securely stored and that data is protected in transit and at rest. Solutions for data loss prevention (DLP) can assist in monitoring and managing the transfer of private information, averting illegal access and exfiltration.

Moreover, thorough incident response procedures are essential for efficiently handling cloud security events. These strategies should specify precise methods for identifying, disclosing, and handling breaches. Employee readiness for handling situations quickly and skillfully can be guaranteed by regular training and simulations. For incident response, working with cloud service providers is particularly crucial since they may offer invaluable resources and assistance in the event of a breach.

Lastly, companies ought to promote a culture of accountability and security awareness. Regular training on cloud security best practices and encouragement to report any questionable activity or vulnerabilities should be provided to staff members. The likelihood of security issues can be significantly decreased by establishing clear policies and processes for cloud security and making sure they are adhered to consistently.

In conclusion, enterprises must learn from actual cloud security incidents to comprehend the possible risks and implement efficient security measures. Case studies that cover companies like Capital One, Verizon, Dow Jones, Exactis, and Uber provide important lessons about managing third-party vendors, protecting sensitive data, securing cloud setups, and keeping incident response transparent. A comprehensive strategy for cloud security may help enterprises protect sensitive data, improve their security posture, and uphold stakeholder and consumer trust.

CHAPTER IX

Future of Cybersecurity

Emerging Technologies and Their Impact

Emerging technologies such as artificial intelligence (AI), machine learning (ML), and blockchain are reshaping cybersecurity. These technologies offer innovative solutions to enhance security measures, detect and mitigate threats, and protect sensitive data. Their applications in cybersecurity are profound, bringing both opportunities and challenges as organizations strive to defend against increasingly sophisticated cyber threats.

AI and ML are revolutionizing cybersecurity by enabling the development of advanced threat detection and response systems. Traditional cybersecurity measures often rely on static rules and signatures, which can be insufficient against dynamic and evolving threats. AI and ML, however, can analyze vast amounts of data in real time, identifying patterns and anomalies that may indicate malicious activity. These technologies use algorithms to learn from historical data, continuously improving their ability to detect and predict threats. For instance, AI-powered security systems can identify previously unknown malware by recognizing unusual behavior rather than relying solely on known signatures.

One of the most significant benefits of AI and ML in cybersecurity is their ability to automate and enhance incident response. AI-driven systems can quickly analyze security incidents, assess their impact, and suggest or implement appropriate responses. This automation reduces the time needed to respond to threats, minimizing potential damage. Furthermore, AI can prioritize alerts based on severity, helping security teams focus on the most critical threats and reducing the burden of false positives. This efficiency is crucial in a landscape where cyber threats are becoming more frequent and complex.

AI and ML also play a crucial role in enhancing endpoint security. Endpoint Detection and Response (EDR) systems incorporating AI can monitor endpoints continuously, detecting and responding to threats in real-time. These systems can identify suspicious activities, such as unusual login patterns or unauthorized access attempts, and take proactive measures to isolate the affected endpoints, preventing the spread of malware or other malicious actions.

However, integrating AI and ML into cybersecurity is challenging. One of the primary concerns is the potential for adversarial attacks, where cybercriminals manipulate AI systems to evade detection or cause incorrect classifications. For example, attackers can use techniques like adversarial machine learning to create data inputs that deceive AI models, making malicious activities appear benign. Addressing these vulnerabilities requires ongoing research and development to enhance the robustness and resilience of AI systems against such attacks.

Blockchain technology is another emerging innovation with significant implications for cybersecurity. Blockchain's decentralized and immutable ledger provides a secure way to record and verify transactions, making it highly resistant to tampering and fraud. This inherent security feature of blockchain is being leveraged in various cybersecurity applications.

One notable application of blockchain in cybersecurity is identity and access management (IAM). Traditional IAM systems are centralized, making them vulnerable to single points of failure and attacks. On the other hand, Blockchain-based IAM solutions use a decentralized approach, distributing identity verification across multiple nodes in the network. This decentralization enhances security by eliminating single points of failure and making it more challenging for attackers to compromise the system. Additionally, blockchain can provide a tamper-proof audit trail of all identity-related transactions, improving transparency and accountability.

Blockchain is also being used to enhance the Internet of Things (IoT) security. IoT devices are often vulnerable to attacks due to their limited processing power and security features. By integrating blockchain with IoT, organizations can create secure, decentralized networks where devices communicate and transact data without relying on a central authority. Blockchain's cryptographic algorithms ensure the integrity and authenticity of data transmitted between IoT devices, reducing the risk of data breaches and unauthorized access.

Another promising application of blockchain in cybersecurity is in supply chain security. Blockchain can provide end-to-end visibility and traceability of goods and materials throughout the supply chain. Each transaction or movement of goods is recorded on the blockchain, creating an immutable record that can be verified by all parties involved. This transparency helps prevent fraud, counterfeiting, and tampering, ensuring the integrity and authenticity of products. Additionally, smart contracts—self-executing contracts with the terms of the agreement directly written into code—can automate and enforce compliance with security standards in the supply chain.

Despite its potential, the adoption of blockchain technology in cybersecurity also faces challenges. Scalability is a significant concern, as the processing power required to maintain and verify blockchain transactions can be substantial, potentially limiting its application in large-scale systems. Moreover, integrating blockchain with existing IT infrastructure can be complex and require significant organizational processes and systems changes. Additionally, while blockchain is highly secure, it is not entirely immune to attacks, such as 51%, where a single entity gains control of most of the network's computing power.

In conclusion, AI, ML, and blockchain are transformative technologies with significant implications for cybersecurity. AI and ML enhance threat detection, incident response, and endpoint security by analyzing vast amounts of data and identifying patterns that indicate malicious activity. However, they also present challenges, such as adversarial attacks that require ongoing research. Blockchain's decentralized and immutable nature offers robust solutions for identity management, IoT security, and supply chain integrity, although its scalability and integration pose challenges. As these technologies continue to evolve, they will play an increasingly critical role in defending against sophisticated cyber threats and ensuring the security of digital ecosystems. Organizations must stay informed about these advancements and integrate them thoughtfully to enhance their cybersecurity posture.

The Role of Quantum Computing

Quantum computing represents a paradigm shift in computational power with profound implications for cybersecurity, offering unprecedented opportunities and significant challenges. Unlike classical computers that process information using bits as either 0s or 1s, quantum computers leverage quantum bits or qubits, which can exist in multiple states simultaneously due to quantum phenomena like superposition and entanglement. This capability enables quantum computers to perform complex calculations exponentially faster than classical computers, potentially revolutionizing fields from cryptography to materials science.

One of the most significant implications of quantum computing for cybersecurity lies in its potential to break traditional cryptographic algorithms that underpin current security protocols. Many encryption schemes used today, such as RSA and ECC (Elliptic Curve Cryptography), rely on the difficulty of factoring large numbers or solving some mathematical issues, which are exponentially faster to solve using quantum algorithms. Once quantum computers achieve a sufficient scale—called quantum supremacy—they could theoretically decrypt sensitive information protected by these algorithms, compromising the confidentiality of data stored and transmitted over the internet.

Researchers are actively developing quantum-resistant algorithms, also known as post-quantum cryptography (PQC), to address this looming threat. These algorithms are designed to withstand attacks from classical and quantum computers, ensuring that sensitive information remains secure in a quantum computing era. PQC research focuses on mathematical problems considered challenging even for quantum computers, such as lattice-based cryptography, hash-based cryptography, and code-based cryptography. Standardization efforts are underway to identify and implement PQC algorithms across various industries and applications to prepare for the quantum computing future.

Beyond its potential to disrupt encryption, quantum computing also offers opportunities to enhance cybersecurity defenses. Quantum technologies can improve the efficiency and accuracy of machine learning algorithms for threat and anomaly detection. Quantum machine learning leverages quantum algorithms to process and analyze vast datasets faster than classical methods, enabling more precise identification of cybersecurity threats in real time. This capability is crucial as cyber threats evolve in complexity and scale.

Moreover, quantum computing holds promise for advancing secure communication protocols, mainly through quantum key distribution (QKD). QKD uses quantum mechanics principles to generate and distribute encryption keys that are inherently secure against eavesdropping attempts, as any attempt to intercept quantum information would disturb the quantum state, alerting the communicating parties. Quantum-secured communication can provide a quantum-safe alternative to traditional cryptographic methods, ensuring the integrity and confidentiality of data transmissions in an era of quantum computing.

In addition to cybersecurity applications, quantum computing has implications for scientific research and technological innovation. Quantum simulations, for instance, can model complex molecular structures and chemical reactions with unprecedented accuracy, accelerating the discovery and development of new materials and pharmaceuticals. Quantum computing's ability to optimize complex systems and algorithms extends to logistics, financial modeling, and optimization problems that underpin many critical business operations.

However, realizing the full potential of quantum computing in cybersecurity and beyond requires overcoming significant technical challenges. Quantum computers are currently in the early stages of development, with existing machines demonstrating only rudimentary capabilities due to the delicate nature of qubits and the need for error correction. Scaling quantum computers to sufficient qubits and achieving error rates low enough for practical applications remains a formidable task. Moreover, quantum computers operate under stringent environmental conditions, such as ultra-low temperatures and isolation from external disturbances, posing additional challenges for deployment and operation.

Preparing for a quantum future involves collaborative efforts across academia, industry, and government to advance quantum research and development. Organizations must invest in quantum-resistant cryptography, develop quantum skills and expertise among cybersecurity professionals, and establish policies and regulations that address the implications of quantum computing for national security and privacy. International cooperation is essential to ensure global standards and norms for quantum technologies, promoting trust and interoperability in a quantum-powered world.

In conclusion, quantum computing represents a disruptive force in cybersecurity with the potential to break traditional encryption algorithms while offering opportunities to enhance security and enable transformative advancements. Developing post-quantum cryptography is critical to mitigating the risks posed by quantum computing ensuring the confidentiality, integrity, and availability of data in a quantum era. Embracing quantum technologies for secure communication and advanced threat detection can bolster cybersecurity defenses and foster innovation across various sectors. As quantum computing continues to evolve, proactive preparation and collaboration will be essential to harnessing its benefits while mitigating potential risks.

Cybersecurity Skills and Workforce Development

Cybersecurity skills and workforce development have become critical issues as organizations face increasingly sophisticated cyber threats worldwide. The rapid evolution of technology, coupled with the growing frequency and complexity of cyber-attacks, has created a significant talent gap in cybersecurity. Addressing this gap requires comprehensive strategies focused on training, education, and fostering a skilled workforce capable of defending against current and future cyber threats.

One of the primary challenges in cybersecurity workforce development is the need for more skilled professionals. According to various industry reports, there is a global shortfall of cybersecurity experts, with estimates suggesting millions of unfilled positions. This shortage is exacerbated by the rapid expansion of digital technologies and the increasing reliance on interconnected systems, which create new vulnerabilities that cybercriminals can exploit. To bridge this gap, organizations, educational institutions, and governments must collaborate to attract, train, and retain talented individuals in the cybersecurity field.

Training and education initiatives play a crucial role in preparing the future cybersecurity workforce. Academic institutions increasingly offer specialized cybersecurity degree programs at the undergraduate and graduate levels. These programs cover many topics, including network security, ethical hacking, incident response, digital forensics, and risk management. Hands-on practical experience through labs, simulations, and internships is integral to these programs, providing students with real-world skills and exposure to industry best practices.

In addition to traditional academic pathways, professional certifications are highly valued in the cybersecurity industry. Certifications such as Certified Information

Systems Security Professional (CISSP), Certified Ethical Hacker (CEH), CompTIA Security+, and others validate expertise and proficiency in specific areas of cybersecurity. Many organizations sponsor employees to pursue these certifications as part of their professional development initiatives, enhancing their skills and knowledge base.

Beyond technical skills, cybersecurity professionals require strong soft skills, such as communication, critical thinking, problem-solving, and collaboration. Effective cybersecurity defense often involves working across teams and departments to implement security measures and respond to incidents promptly. Training programs emphasizing technical and soft skills ensure that cybersecurity professionals are well-rounded and equipped to handle the complexities of modern cyber threats.

Government and industry partnerships are instrumental in advancing cybersecurity workforce development efforts. Governments can incentivize cybersecurity education and training programs, allocate funding for research and development in cybersecurity technologies, and promote cybersecurity career paths through public awareness campaigns. Industry collaboration with academic institutions can help align curriculum with industry needs, provide internship opportunities, and offer mentorship programs to bridge the gap between academia and industry.

Addressing diversity and inclusion in the cybersecurity workforce is also crucial for ensuring a holistic approach to cybersecurity. Diversity brings different perspectives and experiences that can enhance innovation and problem-solving in cybersecurity defense. Initiatives focused on attracting women, minorities, veterans, and individuals from non-traditional backgrounds to cybersecurity careers are essential for building a diverse and resilient workforce.

In conclusion, cybersecurity skills and workforce development are critical components of defending against cyber threats and ensuring the security of digital ecosystems. Training, education, and professional development initiatives are pivotal in preparing the next generation of cybersecurity professionals with the necessary technical expertise, practical experience, and soft skills. Collaborative efforts among governments, educational institutions, industry stakeholders, and professional organizations are essential to address the talent gap, foster innovation, and build a skilled cybersecurity workforce capable of meeting today's and tomorrow's challenges. By investing in cybersecurity education, promoting lifelong learning, and cultivating a diverse and inclusive workforce, organizations can effectively strengthen their defenses and protect against emerging cyber threats.

Global Collaboration and Policy Making

Global collaboration and policy-making in cybersecurity have become increasingly critical as nations and organizations face interconnected and evolving cyber threats. The interconnected nature of the internet means that cyber-attacks can originate from anywhere in the world and target entities across borders, underscoring the need for international cooperation to mitigate risks and strengthen cyber defenses effectively.

One of the primary reasons for the importance of international collaboration in cybersecurity is the transnational nature of cyber threats. Cyber-attacks, such as malware infections, phishing campaigns, and ransomware incidents, often exploit vulnerabilities in global supply chains, critical infrastructure, and digital networks that transcend national boundaries. Addressing these threats requires coordinated efforts among governments, industry stakeholders, and international organizations to share threat intelligence, best practices, and response strategies. Collaborative initiatives, such as information-sharing agreements and joint cybersecurity exercises, enable rapid response and mitigation of cyber incidents on a global scale.

Moreover, cyber threats do not discriminate based on geographical location or political boundaries. Malicious actors can target organizations and individuals in any country, making cybersecurity a shared responsibility that necessitates collective action. By fostering a culture of trust and cooperation among nations, governments can enhance their ability to detect, prevent, and respond to cyber-attacks effectively. International collaboration also facilitates the developing and adoption of global cybersecurity standards and norms, promoting consistency and interoperability in cybersecurity practices across different regions and sectors.

Cybersecurity policy-making at the international level plays a crucial role in shaping cyberspace's regulatory framework and governance mechanisms. Organizations such as the United Nations (UN), International Telecommunication Union (ITU), and the European Union (EU) have established initiatives and frameworks to promote cybersecurity cooperation among member states. These initiatives focus on cybercrime prevention, data protection, incident response coordination, and capacity-building in developing countries. International cybersecurity policies aim to address emerging challenges and ensure a secure and resilient digital environment for global economic and social development by fostering dialogue and consensus-building among diverse stakeholders.

Future trends in cybersecurity policy are likely to emphasize several key areas to strengthen global collaboration and resilience against cyber threats. One trend is the advancement of cross-border legal frameworks and agreements to facilitate international cooperation in combating cybercrime. Mutual legal assistance treaties (MLATs) and extradition agreements enable countries to cooperate in investigating and prosecuting cybercriminals across jurisdictions, ensuring that perpetrators cannot evade justice by exploiting jurisdictional boundaries.

Another trend is the promotion of cybersecurity capacity-building and technical assistance programs, particularly in developing countries and regions with limited cybersecurity infrastructure and expertise. Capacity-building initiatives focus on enhancing the technical skills of cybersecurity professionals, improving national cybersecurity strategies and frameworks, and raising awareness about cyber risks and best practices among businesses and the general public. Countries can strengthen their resilience to cyber threats by investing in cybersecurity capacity-building and contributing to a more secure global digital ecosystem.

Furthermore, adopting risk-based approaches and resilience strategies will likely guide future cybersecurity policies. Risk-based approaches involve prioritizing resources and investments based on cyber threats' likelihood and potential impact on critical infrastructure and essential services. Resilience strategies aim to minimize the impact of cyber incidents by implementing robust incident response plans, conducting regular cyber resilience assessments, and fostering collaboration between the public and private sectors.

Cybersecurity policy-making must also address ethical and human rights considerations concerning privacy protection, data sovereignty, and digital rights. As digital technologies continue to evolve and permeate all aspects of society, policymakers must balance ensuring security and preserving individual liberties and freedoms online. International human rights frameworks and privacy laws, such as the General Data Protection Regulation (GDPR) in the European Union, serve as vital benchmarks for developing inclusive and rights-respecting cybersecurity policies globally.

In conclusion, global collaboration and policy-making are essential for addressing cyber threats' complex and interconnected nature in today's digital world. Countries can enhance their cybersecurity resilience and mitigate risks by promoting international cooperation, sharing threat intelligence, and developing common standards and norms. Future trends in cybersecurity policy will likely focus on strengthening legal frameworks, advancing capacity-building initiatives, integrating emerging technologies, adopting risk-based approaches, and upholding ethical and human rights principles. By embracing these trends and fostering a culture of trust and cooperation, nations can build a more secure and resilient global digital infrastructure for the benefit of all stakeholders.

CHAPTER X

Cybersecurity and the Road Ahead

Recap of Key Points

Throughout this cybersecurity exploration, we've delved into various critical aspects that underscore the importance, challenges, and strategies within cybersecurity. Key themes emerged across different facets of cybersecurity, offering valuable insights and takeaways for organizations and individuals navigating this complex landscape.

A solid understanding of foundational principles and concepts lies at the core of effective cybersecurity. We explored essential terms such as confidentiality, integrity, and availability (CIA), which form the bedrock of cybersecurity strategies. These principles guide the design, implementation, and evaluation of security measures to protect data, systems, and networks from unauthorized access, breaches, and disruptions.

The historical evolution of cybersecurity showcased significant milestones and developments, underscoring how threats have evolved alongside advancements in technology. From the early days of isolated systems to interconnected networks and the pervasive use of the internet, cybersecurity has adapted to combat increasingly sophisticated cyber threats, emphasizing the importance of proactive defense and resilience.

We explored various cyber threats, including malware, phishing, ransomware, and distributed denial-of-service (DDoS) attacks. Case studies highlighted notable cyber incidents that underscored the devastating impact of these threats on organizations and individuals. Understanding the tactics, techniques, and motives behind cyber-attacks is crucial for developing targeted defense strategies and enhancing incident response capabilities.

Frameworks such as the NIST Cybersecurity Framework and global standards provide structured guidelines for organizations to assess and improve their cybersecurity posture. These frameworks emphasize risk management, continuous monitoring, and adaptive security measures tailored to organizational needs and regulatory requirements. Adherence to cybersecurity standards fosters a proactive approach to cybersecurity governance and enhances resilience against evolving threats.

Security Operations Centers (SOCs) are pivotal in detecting, analyzing, and responding to real-time security incidents. Building and maintaining an effective SOC involves deploying advanced technologies, leveraging threat intelligence, and nurturing skilled cybersecurity professionals capable of rapid incident detection and mitigation. The incident response lifecycle, encompassing preparation, detection, containment, eradication, recovery, and lessons learned, guides organizations in effectively managing and recovering from security breaches.

The shift to cloud computing offers scalability, flexibility, and accessibility but introduces unique security challenges. Managing security across hybrid and multi-cloud environments requires robust strategies for data protection, identity, and access management (IAM), and compliance. Organizations must implement specialized tools, such as cloud security posture management (CSPM) and workload protection platforms (CWPP), to mitigate risks and ensure consistent security across diverse cloud platforms.

Ethical considerations in cybersecurity, including responsible disclosure, ethical hacking, and balancing security with privacy rights, underscore the importance of ethical conduct and transparency in cybersecurity practices. Compliance with regulatory frameworks such as GDPR, HIPAA, and industry-specific standards is essential for protecting consumer data, maintaining trust, and avoiding legal liabilities associated with data breaches.

Cybersecurity is a dynamic field that requires continuous improvement, adaptation, and collaboration across organizational boundaries. Embracing a proactive stance towards cybersecurity, investing in employee training, and fostering a culture of security awareness is critical to effectively mitigating emerging threats and evolving risks.

In conclusion, cybersecurity is a multifaceted discipline that demands strategic planning, proactive measures, and continuous vigilance to safeguard assets, mitigate risks, and maintain trust in an interconnected digital landscape. By integrating cybersecurity best practices, leveraging advanced technologies, and fostering a culture of resilience and collaboration, organizations can navigate evolving cyber threats with confidence and resilience. As cybersecurity evolves, staying informed about emerging threats, adopting innovative defenses, and prioritizing cybersecurity as a business imperative are paramount to achieving long-term cybersecurity success in an increasingly interconnected world.

The Evolving Role of Cybersecurity

In today's interconnected digital landscape, cybersecurity plays a pivotal role in safeguarding sensitive data and digital assets, enabling business continuity, maintaining customer trust, and supporting innovation. The role of cybersecurity has evolved significantly from being perceived as a technical function focused on defending against external threats to becoming a strategic imperative that aligns with organizational goals and risk management strategies. This evolution reflects the dynamic nature of cyber threats, technological advancements, and regulatory landscapes, necessitating continuous improvement and adaptation in cybersecurity practices.

Cyber threats continue to evolve in sophistication, frequency, and impact, challenging organizations to stay ahead of malicious actors. Threat actors exploit software, networks, and human behavior vulnerabilities, leveraging social engineering, ransomware, and supply chain attacks to compromise systems and steal valuable information. The evolving threat landscape underscores the importance of proactive threat intelligence, vulnerability management, and incident response capabilities to detect, mitigate, and recover from cyber-attacks effectively.

Cybersecurity is increasingly integrated into business strategy as organizations recognize its pivotal role in protecting intellectual property, maintaining regulatory compliance, and preserving brand reputation. Executives and board members actively engage in cybersecurity governance, ensuring alignment between cybersecurity investments, organizational objectives, and risk appetite. Strategic cybersecurity initiatives focus on enhancing resilience, enabling digital transformation, and fostering a culture of security awareness across all levels of the organization.

Advancements in technology, such as cloud computing, artificial intelligence (AI), and the Internet of Things (IoT), present both opportunities and challenges for cybersecurity. While these technologies enhance operational efficiency and innovation, they also introduce new attack vectors and complexities securing interconnected devices and data streams. Cybersecurity professionals must leverage advanced tools, automated threat detection systems, and machine learning algorithms to identify abnormal behavior, detect insider threats, and respond swiftly to emerging cyber risks.

The regulatory landscape governing cybersecurity continues to evolve globally, with stringent data protection laws such as GDPR in Europe and CCPA in California imposing strict data privacy and security requirements. Compliance with regulatory frameworks necessitates robust data governance practices, transparent data handling procedures, and proactive measures to protect consumer information from unauthorized access or disclosure. Organizations must navigate complex legal obligations, implement data breach notification protocols, and demonstrate accountability for safeguarding sensitive data.

The demand for skilled cybersecurity professionals continues to outpace supply, highlighting the need for workforce development initiatives and talent acquisition strategies. Organizations invest in training programs, certifications, and hands-on experience to cultivate cybersecurity expertise and bridge the skills gap. Collaboration with academic institutions, industry partnerships, and cybersecurity communities fosters knowledge sharing, innovation, and recruitment of diverse talent to strengthen cyber defenses and resilience.

Building a cybersecurity-aware culture is essential for mitigating human error, the leading cause of security incidents. Employees are educated on cybersecurity best practices, phishing awareness, and incident reporting procedures to reduce risks associated with social engineering and insider threats. Leadership commitment to cybersecurity fosters a culture of accountability, transparency, and continuous improvement, empowering employees to prioritize security in their daily activities and decision-making processes.

Cybersecurity will continue to evolve in response to emerging technologies, regulatory changes, and evolving threat landscapes. Future trends include adopting zero-trust security models, enhanced encryption standards, and the integration of cybersecurity into DevOps practices to achieve continuous security testing and automation. Innovations in quantum computing, blockchain technology, and decentralized identity management offer potential solutions to address cybersecurity challenges and enhance resilience against advanced threats.

In conclusion, the evolving role of cybersecurity underscores its strategic importance in safeguarding digital assets, maintaining operational continuity, and enabling digital innovation. Continuous improvement and adaptation are imperative as organizations navigate evolving cyber threats, technological advancements, and regulatory landscapes. By integrating cybersecurity into business strategy, investing in technological solutions, fostering a cybersecurity-aware culture, and cultivating a skilled workforce, organizations can strengthen their cyber defenses, mitigate risks, and embrace opportunities for growth in an increasingly digital and interconnected world. Cybersecurity must be approached collaboratively across departments, industries, and global communities to address current and future cyber challenges and ensure a secure digital future for all stakeholders.

The Promise of a Secure Digital Future

As we navigate an increasingly digital world, the promise of a secure digital future hinges upon our ability to build and maintain a fortified cyber environment that safeguards data, privacy, and critical infrastructure from evolving cyber threats. The rapid proliferation of connected devices, cloud services, and digital platforms has revolutionized how individuals, businesses, and governments operate. Yet, it has also exposed vulnerabilities that malicious actors exploit for financial gain, political motives, or disruption. Achieving a secure digital future requires a concerted effort to integrate robust cybersecurity measures, foster collaboration across sectors, and empower stakeholders with the knowledge and tools to mitigate cyber risks effectively.

Cybersecurity resilience is the foundation of a secure digital future—an organization's ability to anticipate, withstand, and recover from cyber-attacks. This resilience is built upon comprehensive risk management frameworks, proactive threat intelligence, and continuous monitoring of IT environments to detect and respond to threats promptly. By prioritizing cybersecurity resilience, organizations can minimize the impact of cyber incidents, protect sensitive data, and maintain operational continuity in the face of persistent cyber threats.

Advancements in technologies such as artificial intelligence (AI), Internet of Things (IoT), and 5G networks present both opportunities and challenges for cybersecurity. While these technologies drive innovation and enhance connectivity, they also introduce new attack surfaces and vulnerabilities that require advanced security controls and risk mitigation strategies. Securing these emerging technologies involves adopting security-by-design principles, implementing encryption standards, and leveraging AI-driven threat detection to identify and neutralize cyber threats before they escalate.

Regulatory frameworks such as the General Data Protection Regulation (GDPR), California Consumer Privacy Act (CCPA), and industry-specific regulations mandate stringent data protection standards and individual privacy rights. Compliance with these regulations promotes transparency, accountability, and ethical handling of personal data, fostering trust between organizations and their customers. By adhering to regulatory requirements and implementing privacy-by-design principles, organizations can mitigate legal risks, protect consumer privacy, and uphold their commitment to ethical cybersecurity practices.

Innovation is pivotal to advancing cybersecurity capabilities and addressing emerging threats in a rapidly evolving digital landscape. Research and development initiatives focus on developing resilient technologies, encryption methodologies, and threat intelligence platforms that enhance cyber defense capabilities and support proactive risk management strategies. By embracing innovation and fostering a culture of continuous improvement, organizations can stay ahead of cyber adversaries and adapt their security posture to mitigate evolving threats effectively.

Global cybersecurity governance frameworks facilitate international cooperation, standardization of cybersecurity practices, and alignment of regulatory requirements across borders. Organizations collaborate on cybersecurity norms, incident response protocols, and capacity-building initiatives to strengthen global cyber resilience and address transnational cyber threats. By promoting a unified approach to cybersecurity governance, stakeholders can enhance collective cybersecurity capabilities, mitigate geopolitical risks, and foster trust in digital technologies on a global scale.

In conclusion, the promise of a secure digital future hinges upon collective efforts to build a fortified cyber environment that prioritizes resilience, collaboration, and innovation. By integrating robust cybersecurity measures, fostering stakeholder collaboration, and promoting cybersecurity awareness and education, organizations can mitigate cyber risks, protect critical infrastructure, and safeguard digital ecosystems against emerging threats. Embracing a proactive approach to cybersecurity governance, regulatory compliance, and technological innovation empowers stakeholders to navigate the complexities of a digital-first world with confidence, resilience, and a shared commitment to securing our digital future for generations to come.

Final Thoughts and Call to Action

As we conclude our cybersecurity exploration, it is evident that the digital landscape continues to evolve rapidly, presenting unprecedented opportunities and complex challenges. The importance of cybersecurity cannot be overstated, as it underpins trust in digital transactions, protects sensitive data, and preserves the integrity of critical infrastructure. However, achieving robust cybersecurity requires collective responsibility, proactive measures, and unwavering vigilance from individuals, organizations, and governments alike.

Policy and regulatory frameworks are critical in shaping cybersecurity standards, promoting transparency, and holding organizations accountable for safeguarding consumer data and digital assets. Advocating for robust cybersecurity legislation, regulatory compliance, and ethical data practices ensures alignment with global cybersecurity norms and industry best practices. By engaging policymakers, industry stakeholders, and cybersecurity experts in dialogue, stakeholders can influence legislative agendas, shape regulatory frameworks, and advance cybersecurity governance initiatives that enhance digital trust and resilience.

Investing in cybersecurity education, training, and workforce development initiatives is essential for addressing the growing demand for skilled cybersecurity professionals. By promoting STEM education, cybersecurity certifications, and hands-on training programs, stakeholders can cultivate a diverse talent pipeline equipped with the knowledge and skills to tackle emerging cyber threats and innovate within cybersecurity. Empowering the next generation of cybersecurity professionals strengthens cyber defenses, fosters innovation, and ensures sustainable cybersecurity resilience for years.

Cybersecurity is a dynamic and evolving field that requires continuous learning, adaptation, and innovation to stay ahead of evolving cyber threats. Encouraging a culture of continuous improvement and adaptive security measures enables organizations to anticipate emerging threats, implement proactive defenses, and respond effectively to cyber incidents. By embracing technological advancements, adopting best practices, and investing in cybersecurity research and development, stakeholders can drive innovation and shape the future of cybersecurity in an increasingly digital and interconnected world.

In conclusion, cybersecurity is a shared responsibility that demands proactive measures, unwavering vigilance, and collective action from individuals, organizations, and governments worldwide. By embracing proactive cybersecurity measures, promoting cybersecurity vigilance and awareness, fostering collaboration and information sharing, driving policy and regulatory initiatives, empowering the next generation of cybersecurity professionals, and inspiring a culture of continuous improvement, stakeholders can contribute to a secure digital future. Together, we can navigate the complexities of the digital age, mitigate cyber risks, and safeguard our digital ecosystems for generations. Let us take action today to build a resilient and fortified cyber environment that fosters trust, innovation, and prosperity in the digital era.

CONCLUSION

As we conclude "The Promise of Cybersecurity: From Prevention to Response: Building a Fortified Cyber Environment," it is clear that cybersecurity is an ever-evolving field that requires continuous vigilance and adaptation. This book has journeyed through the critical aspects of cybersecurity, from understanding the threat landscape to implementing robust prevention and response strategies.

We have explored the foundational principles and advanced techniques necessary to protect our digital environments. By delving into real-world case studies and examining emerging technologies, we have gained insights into the complexities and dynamics of cybersecurity. The importance of a well-structured incident response plan, the necessity of compliance with legal standards, and the ethical considerations have all been emphasized to build a comprehensive understanding.

The cybersecurity landscape will be shaped by new technologies, evolving threats, and global cooperation. The promise of cybersecurity lies in our ability to stay ahead of these changes, ensuring that our defenses are as dynamic as the threats we face. We can build a fortified cyber environment by fostering a culture of security awareness, investing in continuous education, and embracing innovative solutions.

This book serves as a call to action for all stakeholders—individuals, organizations, and governments—to commit to robust cybersecurity practices. Together, we can achieve the promise of a secure digital future where the benefits of technology are enjoyed without compromising our safety and privacy.

Thank you for buying and reading/ listening to our book. If you found this book useful/ helpful please take a few minutes and leave a review on the platform where you purchased our book. Your feedback matters greatly to us.

www.ingramcontent.com/pod-product-compliance
Lightning Source LLC
Chambersburg PA
CBHW071218050326
40689CB00011B/2360